THE GRAIN BRAIN COOKBOOK

Also by Dr David Perlmutter

Grain Brain
Power Up Your Brain
Raise a Smarter Child by Kindergarten
The Better Brain Book

THE GRAIN BRAIN
COOKBOOK

More Than 150 Life-Changing Gluten-Free
Recipes to Transform Your Health

DR DAVID PERLMUTTER

First published in Great Britain in 2014 by Yellow Kite
An imprint of Hodder & Stoughton
An Hachette UK company

First published in the US in 2014 by Little, Brown and Company

1

A CIP catalogue record for this title is available from the British Library

Trade Paperback ISBN 978 1 473 61917 3
eBook ISBN 978 1 473 61916 6

Typeset by Palimpsest Book Production Limited, Falkirk, Stirlingshire

Printed and bound by Clays Ltd, St Ives plc

Hodder & Stoughton policy is to use papers that are natural, renewable and
recyclable products and made from wood grown in sustainable forests.
The logging and manufacturing processes are expected to conform
to the environmental regulations of the country of origin.

Hodder & Stoughton Ltd
338 Euston Road
London NW1 3BH

www.hodder.co.uk

This book is dedicated to our daughter, Reisha, for helping me embrace the beauty of our world, to our son, Austin, who restores my faith in and devotion to the practice of medicine, and to my wife, Leize, whose love, understanding, and companionship have sustained and supported me on our incredible journey together.

Contents

Introduction

Welcome to a New Way of Life

Let food be thy medicine and medicine be thy food.
— Hippocrates, the father of modern medicine

Several years ago our beloved terrier Teako began losing his fur, and my wife and I decided to take him to the veterinarian. The first question the vet asked in the exam room was simply, "What are you feeding your dog?" As my wife responded, I was struck by that insightful question. Few of us are surprised when our vet asks what we are feeding our pets because we readily accept the notion that the foods they consume have a significant role in their health and wellness (and, conversely, risk for illness and disease). What dawned on me was the thought of how unusual it is for a doctor to similarly ask an ailing human patient, "What are you *eating?*" No doubt, most people would be taken aback by such a question, and some might even consider it offensive. They expect queries about their medications and symptoms, not inquiries about their dietary choices. Sadly, they also anticipate more drugs to add to their daily regimen, with no mention of what kinds of modifications they could be making in their eating and lifestyle habits to treat their health conditions.

Food matters. I believe that what we eat is the most important decision we make every day in terms of health and our ability to resist and combat disease. I also believe that the shift in our diet that has occurred over the past century—from high-fat, low-carb to today's low-fat, high-carb trend, fundamentally consisting of grains and other damaging carbohydrates—is at the root of many of the modern scourges linked to the brain, including chronic headaches, insomnia, anxiety, depression, epilepsy, movement disorders, schizophrenia, attention deficit hyperactivity disorder (ADHD), and those senior moments that quite likely herald serious cognitive decline and full-blown, irreversible, untreatable, and incurable brain disease.

The idea that our brain is sensitive to what we eat has been quietly circulating in our most prestigious medical literature recently. And what cutting-edge research is finally revealing, to the bewilderment of many, is that the human brain is far more responsive to nutritional choices than we ever imagined. While it's common knowledge now that "heart smart" diets can help support the cardiovascular system, and that we can prevent osteoporosis by getting plenty of calcium and vitamin D in our diets, it's not universally appreciated yet that we can indeed affect the fate of our brain's health—for better or worse—by what we put in our mouths. Hippocrates got it right thousands of years ago when he said that food should be our medicine and medicine our food.

I covered this topic at length in my 2013 book *Grain Brain*, in which I detail how and why food impacts brain health. And I devote a lot of space in that book to explaining that we can employ the power of nutrition to prevent what's perhaps our most dreaded brain condition of all—Alzheimer's disease, an affliction for which there is no meaningful remedy whatsoever. A bold, aggressive statement to make, I know, but the science is finally here to show how this is possible. In 2010, the *New England Journal of Medicine* published a new study showing that the costs for dementia care in 2010 were estimated to be as high as $200 billion, roughly twice that expended for heart disease and almost triple what was spent on cancer. By some estimates, 2.7 million Alzheimer's patients in America today might not have developed this disease, which robs its victims of their ability to respond to the world around them, if only they and their families had learned that food matters. If only my father, once a renowned neurosurgeon, had known this decades ago before his own brain plunged down the path to advanced Alzheimer's. Indeed, my mission is deeply personal. But it isn't just about ending Alzheimer's disease.

PREVENTION IS THE CURE

I've been a practicing neurologist for the past thirty-odd years, dealing with a wide array of brain disorders and dementia on a daily basis. I work in a medical system that's unfortunately still trying to treat patients with strong drugs rather than cure them through prevention. In today's world, we're told that we can pretty much live our lives, come what may—and then, if our health is affected, we just turn to our doctors to provide us with "magic pills" that (hopefully) alleviate the problem. But you often can't take a pill to cure a brain condition. And while drugs exist to address symptoms, they won't necessarily eradicate the source of the problem. This is true whether we're talking about anxiety or migraines, depression or dementia.

One of the examples I highlight in *Grain Brain* is the incidence of "ADHD" in this country, which shows just how reactive rather than proactive we've become in healthcare. In the past decade, the ADHD diagnosis has increased 53 percent. I'm not convinced ADHD is a medical condition that should be treated with powerful drugs; I think this increase is almost certainly due to what we're feeding our children. But the medical establishment too often convinces parents that medication is the best "quick fix." Eighty-five percent of all ADHD medications produced in the world are used exclusively in the U.S., a sobering statistic. A full 11 percent of all American children now carry this diagnosis—that's *6.4 million American children* ages four through seventeen. By definition, these metrics clearly qualify ADHD as an epidemic here in the U.S. More heart-wrenching is the fact that an incredible two-thirds of those children are now on medication for a problem that may have been completely preventable (and may be reversible using diet alone). Clearly, there is something wrong with this picture. Something is happening to our brains.

Let me give you one more example. About 10 percent of America's adult population suffers from depression, a statistic that qualifies this condition as an epidemic as well. And while we normally don't think of depression as a "serious" illness, it's directly associated with approximately 30,000 deaths in this country every year. Depression is almost always treated with potent pills—drugs that change the natural chemistry of the body and brain and come with many side effects. Antidepressants, in fact, are among the most prescribed drugs in America, fueling a multi-billion dollar industry.

But as I've already stated (and as I describe in detail in *Grain Brain*), depression, Alzheimer's disease, and ADHD, among other brain-related ailments, can be prevented through the diet. The various medications prescribed for these issues focus squarely on symptoms, basically treating the smoke while ignoring the fire. I argue we need to focus on the fire itself: *inflammation*.

YOUR #1 VILLAIN: THE SILENT KILLER

Contrary to what you might think, the inflammatory process that's involved in the degeneration in your arthritic knee or your coronary arteries is the very same one that leads to the deterioration of the human brain. Your arthritic knee is painful because it's inflamed. So what do you do? If you're like most people, you reach for an anti-inflammatory medication to put the fire out. And that's exactly what we need to do in the brain. But that doesn't mean taking a medication; it means creating an environment in which the fire never burns in the first place. That's the cornerstone of preventing every brain-related condition or disorder. As John Kennedy said, "The time to repair the roof is when the sun is shining."

Researchers have known for some time that the essence of all degenerative conditions, including brain disorders, is inflammation. But until now, scientists didn't know the instigators of that inflammation—the first missteps that prompt this deadly reaction. And what we are finding is that gluten (a protein found in wheat, barley, and rye) and a high carbohydrate diet are among the most prominent stimulators of inflammatory pathways that reach the brain. What's most disturbing about this discovery is that we often don't know when our brains are being negatively affected. Digestive disorders and food allergies are much easier to spot because symptoms such as gas, bloating, pain, constipation, and diarrhea emerge relatively quickly. But the brain is a more elusive organ. It could be enduring assaults at a molecular level without your feeling it. Unless you're nursing a headache or managing an obvious neurological problem, it can be hard to know what's going on in the brain until it's too late. And once the diagnosis is in for brain disease, it's difficult to turn the train around.

Although the influence of inflammation on brain health and disease is widespread, the upside is that our food choices can directly impact inflammation. And when you consider inflammation's role in cancer, diabetes, heart disease, obesity, and virtually every other chronic condition common in Western cultures, the implications of what you eat are nothing short of life changing. I'm going to show you how to control your genetic destiny through your diet—even if you were born with a genetic tendency to develop a neurological challenge.

This will require you to free yourself from a few myths that many people still cling to: 1) carbs are good; and 2) fat is bad.

(It's beyond the scope of this book to go into further detail about inflammation—what exactly it is, how it can become problematic in a human body, how we test for it, and so on. I examine inflammation in greater depth in *Grain Brain*, and I encourage you to go there for more information. It's a topic on which everyone should be more informed.)

THE BLOOD SUGAR CONNECTION: WHY YOU MUST GO LOW CARB

If you live to be 85 years old, and you do *nothing to change your risk for brain disease today*, you have a 50/50 chance of developing Alzheimer's disease. That's a mere flip of a coin. If you have a family history of Alzheimer's disease, your risk is dramatically increased. And if you're a type 2 diabetic, your risk is *doubled*. Now, you obviously can't change your family history, but type 2 diabetes is often an outcome of poor lifestyle choices.

The idea that your risk for Alzheimer's is tied to diabetes may seem inconceivable at first. But it makes sense when you consider the relationships shared between these two ailments. Diabetes is characterized by elevated blood sugar. And elevated blood sugar is directly toxic to brain cells. In a recent report in the top journal *Neurology*, researchers studied 266 healthy adults who had no cognitive difficulties. First, the researchers measured their fasting blood sugar, a test to determine how much sugar (glucose) was in their bloodstream and how well they metabolized sugar. Next, each member of the group had an MRI scan that looked at the size of two regions of the brain involved with cognitive function and memory: the hippocampus and the amygdala. The researchers then had these same individuals come back to the laboratory four years later to repeat the MRI scans. Their findings were breathtaking. The scientists found a striking correlation between average blood sugar levels and the degree of shrinkage of these two brain parts. The higher a person's blood sugar levels, even within the "normal" range, the higher the degree of shrinkage. The scientists calculated the blood sugar to be responsible for 6–10 percent of the size reductions, even after factoring in other potential causes such as alcohol consumption, smoking, age, and high blood pressure.

This is empowering information, telling us that higher blood sugar levels translate directly to more aggressive brain shrinkage, specifically in areas that determine our cognitive and memory function. And so-called "normal" blood sugar levels—or what we think is normal—*are not good enough* if you want to preserve your brain and mental faculties. Make no mistake about it: your blood sugar levels are a reflection of your consumption of carbohydrates and sugars. This knowledge is what informs every recipe you're about to explore.

In August of 2013, a similar study was published in the *New England Journal of Medicine* that further confirmed the indelible link between blood sugar levels and brain health. This latest investigation documented fasting blood sugars in a group of 2,067 elderly individuals. Although some of these individuals had diabetes at the start, most them did not, and none had dementia in the beginning. Over a follow-up period of almost seven years, the researchers also had participants perform mental examinations to gauge their cognitive strength. They found a nearly perfect correlation between levels of blood sugar and risk for dementia. Those with higher average blood sugar levels within the preceding five years had a statistically significant increased risk for dementia. This held true whether one started with diabetes or not.

Clearly, maintaining healthy levels of blood sugar is an important part of keeping your brain on cue as you age. The recipes throughout this book are designed to help you do just that. But we're not aiming to have just "good" blood sugar control; we're seeking excellent, total control. And the way you can achieve that control is to cut back on your carbohydrates, including plain sugar and foods that contain starches (such as breads, pastas, and potatoes). You can make healthy substitutions for all of these foods—substitutions that are just as tasty and satisfying, if not more so. I'll give you plenty of ideas about how to do this, with suggestions such as adding more non-starchy vegetables like mixed greens and peppers to your plate, or trying my creative recipes that include nuts and seeds. For example, sautéed spinach with garlic and toasted pumpkin seeds is delicious, packed with nutrients, and will help manage blood sugar.

It's not always easy to understand where sugars and carbohydrates are coming from. A 350-ml (12-fl oz) glass of orange juice, for instance, is typically looked upon as being a healthy choice. This drink has become a staple in the American diet, but it contains a whopping 36 grams of sugar. That's nine teaspoons of sugar, about the same found in a can of regular cola.

At breakfast, many of us are bombarding our bodies with high levels of brain-damaging carbohydrates without even realizing it. Down your glass of orange juice, have a bowl of whole grain cereal with a banana, maybe eat a croissant or wholemeal toast with jam . . . and you've just set the stage for elevated blood sugar levels that may very well lead to your brain's demise farther down the road. Like orange juice, fruit itself represents a significant source of carbohydrates in the typical American diet. To be clear, it's perfectly reasonable to have a handful of blueberries or an apple a day, but the 4 to 6 servings that are often recommended by "health experts" may wreak havoc with your body's ability to process sugar.

Our goal is to keep total daily carbohydrates at or below 60 to 80 grams per day. (This certainly casts that glass of orange juice, which has about half of that daily carb load, in a new light.) If you follow the recipes in this book, you won't have to count carbs during your day. Here's what 60 to 80 grams of carbohydrates looks like. It means having an incredibly tasty, nutrient-packed breakfast of a spinach and onion omelette covered in extra virgin olive oil, sliced avocado, and lemon juice. It means a great salad at lunch with walnuts, olives, goat cheese, and more olive oil for added fat. And how about baked salmon for dinner with broccoli, mushrooms, and a crunchy walnut rocket salad?

If there's one thing about my diet protocol that sets it apart from others, it's that it derives a lot of flavors from fat. That's right: fat. Along with a substantial reduction in carb consumption, the very best thing you can do for your brain is to bring wonderful, healthful, life-sustaining fat back into your kitchen. Dietary fat is what we've been eating for 2.6 million years, and it's exceedingly important, vital for the health of every cell in your body.

A FAT DIET THAT CAN MAKE YOU SMART (AND SLENDER)

If you haven't read *Grain Brain*, you may be surprised by how much fat you'll be welcoming into your kitchen using these recipes. Dietary fat, demonized over the last several decades, is actually a super-fuel for the brain. Leading scientists now confirm that *more* fat in the diet is the way to go to ensure a healthy brain. My hope is that as you experience these delicious recipes, you'll reconnect with a love for fat, a fundamental food choice for health and longevity. And you'll learn what makes for healthful choices in the fats you reintroduce to your cooking.

Look around. Our diets have obviously changed in the past several decades—while at the same time, death from brain diseases has increased dramatically. From 1979 to 2010, the number of deaths related to brain diseases in America increased by an incredible 66 percent in men and 92 percent in women. These numbers are much higher than those in other Western countries, yet we are in no way genetically different from members of other countries. The difference lies in our food choices, and what those choices are doing to us physically.

For most of human evolution, we've eaten what we could either find or kill (until modern agriculture and manufacturing made food acquisition practically effortless). And in terms of getting enough calories to survive, fat has always been our friend. It's an optimal fuel for the human body, and it's by far and away the supreme fuel for the brain.

Let's turn to some landmark science to prove this fact, since I realize some of you may be scratching your heads. A two-year study published in 2008 in the *New England Journal of Medicine* followed 322 adults who were randomly placed on one of three different diets: low-carb, low-fat, or Mediterranean. (Like the low-carb diet, the Mediterranean diet emphasizes healthy fats like olive oil and fish, nuts and seeds, and whole fruits and vegetables, but allows for more carbs through whole grains.) The low-carb and Mediterranean diets showed the greatest weight loss, 5.5 kg (12 lb) and 4.6 kg (10 lb), respectively. The researchers looked at a variety of parameters that have an important impact on health, such as weight and signs of inflammation. The study also revealed that those on the low-carb (high-fat) diet had a much higher level of HDL, so-called "good cholesterol," compared to the low-fat dieters. Triglycerides, which are a fatty substance in blood, are a huge risk factor for coronary artery disease. Those people on the low-fat diet consuming the highest level of carbohydrates had almost no change in their triglycerides, while the drop in triglycerides in those on the high-fat, low-carb diet was almost *ten-fold* greater.

But even more importantly, the study demonstrated that the presence of a biomolecule called C-reactive protein, a famous marker for inflammation, was sizably lowered only in those individuals who *ate the most fat*. The high fat consumers had the lowest levels of C-reactive protein, meaning less inflammation. Here's where the science is even more compelling. A 2012 report from the Mayo Clinic published in the *Journal of Alzheimer's Disease* showed that the risk of becoming demented was reduced by an astounding 44 percent in people eating a high-fat, low-carb diet compared to those who ate lower levels of fat. Those favoring the most carbs in their diets actually experienced an *increased* risk for dementia by a whopping 89 percent.

Not all fats are created equal, however. And I'm not saying *being* fat is a good thing. You shouldn't be eating any trans fats or making excuses to eat a pastry or cook with corn oil because they contain fat. What you find in prepared, low-fat, high-carbohydrate foods at the grocery store and in many of the cooking oils that sit on the shelf month after month are the highly modified fats that damage the brain (and will make you fat).

Hence, your diet should be rich in healthy sources of life-giving fat like:

- extra virgin olive oil
- coconut oil
- avocado
- grass-fed beef
- wild-caught fish (not the farm-raised salmon or sea bass you see in some supermarkets)
- nuts (e.g., almonds, walnuts, pecans)
- seeds (e.g., pumpkin seeds)

It's ideal to choose grass-fed beef rather than grain-fed for a couple of reasons. One, grass-fed beef is naturally rich in brain-healthy omega-3 fats that reduce inflammation. The meat from grain-fed cattle contains far higher levels of omega-6 fats that actually cause inflammation. What's more, these animals generally receive GMO strains of feed and may well have been treated with hormones and antibiotics.

I also encourage you to eat more of nature's perfect food: eggs! These 70-calorie nutrient bombs have all of the essential amino acids we need to survive, plus vitamins, minerals, and brain-protective antioxidants. They also contain an ingredient that's associated with a more than 70 percent reduced risk of dementia in the elderly. Moreover, it's a fundamental component of every cell membrane in your body, and the precursor for all the steroid hormones in the body and even vitamin D. This "ingredient" is cholesterol, something you've probably been trying to avoid for years now.

Cholesterol is one of the most important biochemicals for healthy brain function and indeed for human health in general. Cholesterol is so vital for brain health that even though the brain represents only about 2 to 3 percent of your body weight, 25 percent of the entire cholesterol content of your body is in your brain, where it performs critical roles to facilitate the brain's complex operations. It also strengthens, nourishes, and protects brain cells, and helps clear away harmful free radicals.

The current war on cholesterol, especially as it relates with cardiovascular disease and risk for heart attack, is absolutely unfounded. We desperately need cholesterol in order to be healthy. In fact, every cell in your body manufactures cholesterol because it's so essential. Research has already proven that people with the lowest levels of cholesterol have a significantly higher risk for depression, suicide, and, in the elderly, dementia and even death. Some research indicates that in folks aged 85 or older, higher cholesterol is associated with extraordinary *resistance* to dementia. And yet, the pharmaceutical industry would have you believe that cholesterol is your enemy and that you should do everything you can, including taking powerful drugs, to lower the amount of this pivotal chemical. In my professional opinion, it's rarely, if ever, appropriate to consider high cholesterol alone to be a significant threat to health if you're engaging in a healthy lifestyle that limits the true drivers of cardiovascular disease—smoking, excess alcohol consumption, lack of aerobic exercise, overweight, and a diet high in carbohydrates. In fact, the best lab report to refer to in determining your health status is not cholesterol levels; it's hemoglobin A1C, a snapshot of your average blood sugar level over the previous three months. The higher your A1C level, regardless of cholesterol, the higher your risk for brain disease. When you talk to your doctor about these ideas (and you absolutely should), be prepared for responses that are founded in his or her emotions and not in current science. (See *Grain Brain* for more facts and for a comprehensive discussion of this topic.)

Since cholesterol plays such a crucial role in health, and specifically brain health, we have to revamp our notions about what constitutes a good diet. We've all been told that we shouldn't eat eggs because they are high in cholesterol and saturated fat. But in 2013, the medical journal *Metabolism* published an incredible report evaluating the results of blood tests from people who eat eggs versus egg substitutes. The researchers found that those who ate real eggs actually *had improvement* in various blood tests that measure health in terms of risk for cardiovascular disease, diabetes, and brain disorders. The truth is that we've been eating saturated fat for over 2 million years. And the science is now showing that saturated fat is *not* the culprit in terms of heart disease. It's the sugar and carbohydrates.

What matters most in terms of your diet is that you lower carbohydrates and increase healthy fats. I encourage my patients to eat lean, grass-fed beef, pasture-raised poultry, dairy, and egg yolks—all of which contain cholesterol. It's good for them. It's good for all of us.

THE WHOLE GRAIN TRUTH: WHY YOU MUST DITCH GLUTEN

As I just described, ongoing inflammation plays a major role in compromising brain health and function. And many things can trigger inflammatory processes in the body: injury and illness due to an invading germ or virus, chronic conditions like cancer, obesity, and anxiety, environmental factors like smoking, pollution, and poor sleep, or a food ingredient to which the immune system adversely reacts. One of my main messages in *Grain Brain* is about the deleterious effect that a particular protein called gluten can have on the body. As the name implies, it's like glue. Gluten is the sticky stuff that allows us to make pizza dough, bread, pasta, and pastries. But our physiology was never designed to deal with this relatively new and very strange protein. When our bodies encounter something foreign and unusual, we typically mount an immune response. And that means inflammation.

Over the past decade researchers around the world have begun to discover that being sensitive to gluten can substantially increase inflammation throughout the human body. This is frightening because gluten is in a lot of the food we're eating today—anything made with wheat, barley, or rye. And what makes it even worse is that gluten is frequently found in the very foods we're told are "healthy," such as whole grains. Every day we read claims made on foods and in advertising about "whole grain goodness." At the same time, we hear about the benefits of low-fat this or that, and we conclude that we should be avoiding fat and embracing whole grain.

I'm going to assume that you're already somewhat familiar with gluten and the trend in going gluten-free, as it's made a lot of headlines in the past couple of years. (Again, for an in-depth exploration of this topic, see *Grain Brain*.) The reason it's receiving so much attention now is because the science is very compelling, especially as it relates to brain health. To clarify, I'm not just talking about celiac disease, a rare autoimmune disorder whereby individuals have a unique sensitivity to gluten that involves their small intestine. I'm talking about a type of gluten sensitivity that may affect up to 30 percent of us, which has been linked to a variety of neurological problems beyond dementia, including movement disorders, epilepsy, and muscle disorders. It has also been linked to conditions such as ADHD, depression, headaches, migraines, damage to the nerves (called neuropathy), and even schizophrenia.

As soon as the neurological community began to recognize inflammation as the root cause of a vast array of brain conditions, I began testing virtually every one of my patients for gluten sensitivity, whether they were complaining of headaches or memory lapses.

The results were eye-opening, as I witnessed my patients improve from longstanding conditions just by going gluten-free. People who'd been plagued by chronic neurological disorders from crushing migraines and epilepsy to relentless anxiety and depression were suddenly freed from their conditions. So I began to evangelize to anyone who would listen—patients and colleagues alike—about the importance not only of a low carbohydrate diet, but also of screening for gluten sensitivity and getting people who are gluten sensitive on a gluten-free diet. These are the most powerful interventions I have learned in my thirty years of practicing medicine.

At this point, I know what you're asking: Haven't we always consumed wheat (and therefore gluten)? Our consumption of wheat as a grain actually began about 10,000 years ago, with the advent of agriculture. Prior to that, wheat was not available, and it's not as if our hunter-gatherer forebears suddenly stumbled upon a wheat field. So when I say that we've been consuming wheat for the past 10,000 years, it might seem like a long time to many people. In reality, though, for more than 99 percent of our time on this planet we've been essentially wheat and gluten free.

And why is this important? Our genes are pretty much exactly the same as they have been for at least the past 50,000 years, and these are the genes that dictate which foods we can tolerate. Genetically, we are not prepared to eat wheat—an ingredient that now makes up 20 percent of all calories that we as humans consume. With devastating consequences.

To many, bashing wheat and gluten is almost sacrilegious. We're told "give us this day our daily bread." And whether it's matzoh, the unleavened bread eaten at the Jewish holiday of Passover, or the wafers representing the body of Christ given at communion, you can see why some people may consider this blasphemy. And what about the expression "the greatest thing since sliced bread"? Truth be told, brain disease starts with your daily bread.

The wheat consumed in biblical times is not representative of what passes for wheat today, which is subject to aggressive hybridization. Today's wheat renders a product that our physiology cannot process. And as you know by now, when you challenge your body with foods that it cannot recognize, you're creating the perfect storm to increase inflammation.

It's essential to understand that our food is more than just the macronutrients of fat, protein, and carbohydrates, or the micronutrients like minerals and vitamins. Food is information, and it actually plays an important role in controlling our DNA. It's true: the expression of your genes is dictated by the foods you choose to eat.

We can eat foods that turn on certain genes, genes that then make chemicals that increase inflammation. Or we can choose to eat foods that fundamentally reduce inflammation and increase our body's genetically programmed production of antioxidants that protect us from the ravaging effects of inflammation. You can control your genetic destiny through diet and lifestyle—it's as simple as that. The key thing to remember is that the ultimate goal is to control inflammation. And this is achieved through my dietary protocol, which has the power to reduce inflammation directly and indirectly by supporting a healthy expression of genes related to longevity and anti-inflammatory pathways.

THE *GRAIN BRAIN* DIET

Last year an 80-year-old Italian woman was brought into my office by her two sons because she was failing mentally. She hadn't yet been formally diagnosed with Alzheimer's, but she was unable to follow a conversation and was even beginning to have problems with everyday tasks such as dressing and preparing meals. She had been to a brain specialist who prescribed a medicine that, according to her sons, had only made things worse (which I have to admit is actually very common). We ultimately found that she was sensitive to gluten but had no intestinal distress or celiac disease. At that point I put her on a gluten-free, low-carbohydrate, higher fat diet. Within a few weeks, one of her sons described her transformation bluntly: "It's as if she's awakened, and we have our mom back." This is treating the fire, the cause of a problem, not just the smoke. And this is my wish for you on the *Grain Brain* diet. Even if you're not currently harboring a fire within, this diet will have a profound impact on how your body's computer—your brain—will be working next year, in five years, and really, for the rest of your life.

I realize how hard it is for many people to give up their beloved bread, pasta, and desserts, but what follows are recipes that will give you the keys to the kingdom: Delicious, low-carb, high-fat, and gluten-free meal plans. I suggest that you follow the four-week program that I outline in *Grain Brain*, which will help you ease into this new lifestyle. Of course, it's good practice to check with your physician before beginning any new diet regimen, particularly if you have existing health issues, such as diabetes or heart disease.

Once you begin to follow my dietary guidelines and use the recipes in this book, you will achieve some pretty important goals relatively quickly. You'll shift your body away from relying on carbohydrates for fuel, cut cravings for sugar, feel energized (and hopefully gravitate to more exercise), move into a restful sleep pattern, and establish a new rhythm for long-term, healthy living.

Making dietary changes, even small ones, can seem overwhelming at first. You wonder how you can avoid your usual habits and favorite foods. Will you feel deprived and hungry? Will you find it impossible to keep this new lifestyle up forever? I can hear you already: "How can I go without a slice of pizza?" "How can I ever eat in a restaurant?" "How do I celebrate with family and friends?" "But life without sweets is not possible!"

Believe me, I've heard it all. My answer to these laments is very straightforward. This is not punishment; it is the path to great health and enjoyment. The sooner you experience the rewards of this diet, the sooner you'll never think about pizza and pastries again (nor crave them). Just like everyone else, I go to parties, attend conferences, and celebrate events that put me face to face with the enemy. But I never find myself negotiating whether or not to eat that pie or reach for the bread basket. The thought never crosses my mind. And it won't for you either once you take the initial plunge and feel the effects.

Most of us eat out several times a week, especially while we're at work, so it's imperative that we learn how to navigate other menus while sticking with this protocol. And it's actually easier than you'd initially think. The guidelines in this cookbook will allow you to make healthful food choices when dining out or traveling. Although the meat may not be grass-fed or the chicken pasture-raised, and though the vegetables may be non-organic, there is usually plenty to eat that is low-carb and free of gluten, and you can easily pass on those foods that are not. It's not that hard to make any menu work for you as long as you're savvy about your decisions. Restaurants usually offer meats and fish that can be cooked to your liking, and nowadays the side dishes are often ordered separately. Baked fish with steamed vegetables is likely to be a safe bet (hold the potatoes, fries, and bread basket, and ask for a side salad with olive oil and vinegar). Watch out for elaborate dishes that contain multiple ingredients. And when in doubt, ask your server or the chef about the dishes. Once you get used to using the recipes in this book, you'll find it much easier to know what to order when you're out, as well as what to request in terms of substitutes so you can stay within the confines of the diet.

You'd be surprised by what a little experimentation in the kitchen can do to turn a classic dish filled with gluten and inflammatory ingredients into an equally delicious but brain-friendly meal. Instead of regular flour or wheat, you'll use coconut flour, nut meals like ground almonds, and ground flaxseed; in lieu of sugar, you'll sweeten the recipe with stevia or small amounts of whole fruits (until you're ready to fully disconnect yourself from sweets); and rather than cook with processed vegetable oils, you'll stick with old-fashioned butter and extra virgin olive oil.

And when you're faced with temptation (the box of doughnuts at work or a friend's birthday cake), remind yourself that you'll pay for the indulgence. Be willing to accept those consequences if you cannot say no. A grain-brain-free way of life is, in my humble opinion, the most fulfilling and gratifying way of life there is. Enjoy it.

As you'll soon discover, I've gathered a terrific selection of recipes that will make your move into a healthier way of life absolutely stress free in the kitchen. These meals are easy to prepare, fun to serve, and downright delicious to eat. The additional bonus is that as you spend time in your own kitchen cooking these wonderful dishes, you will see the weight fall off and, should you choose to have them, laboratory tests will show vast improvements in many areas of your biochemistry. Perhaps most importantly, if your brain could talk out loud, you would hear it say that it is happy and functioning at its highest level. Aren't those good enough reasons to say goodbye to gluten and most carbohydrates, and say hello to healthy fat? I think so, and I think you will, too, once you've tasted how good the *Grain Brain* diet can be.

The Grain Brain Pantry

IF YOU'RE FAMILIAR WITH MY BOOK *Grain Brain*, you know what lies ahead. No more bread, pasta, pastry, sushi, soy, or sugars. Even those products labeled gluten-, fat-, or sugar-free are banished. But don't panic: that's where this cookbook is here to help. I'm going to show you how you can conquer your cravings for sugar, wheat, and addictive carbs while still eating with enormous satisfaction and gaining optimal health. You'll quickly know that it is worth the effort as you spend your days with clearer thoughts, better sleep, and renewed energy.

As you begin your new way of life in the kitchen, I suggest that you learn to grocery shop with a shopping list in hand when you are *not* hungry. This prevents spur-of-the-moment and usually not-good-for-you purchases. You'll find that most healthy foods (fresh produce, meats, and dairy) are located around the perimeter of the grocery store while the "bad guys" (pre-packaged, processed foods) are usually in the middle aisles, so steer clear of those toxic areas. Health food stores can often be just as harmful in the prepared foods and packaged foods that they offer. To me, your best bet is your local farmers' market where you are almost always assured that the vegetables are grown free of pesticides and other potentially harmful growth aids, and the meat, poultry, and fish come as nature intended. Of course, I do understand that shopping in this way can be expensive, but I think spending a little extra money to splurge on brain-friendly nutrition is worth it. The old adage "pay me now or pay me later" is extremely relevant here, for if you don't spend money on good nutrition today, you'll be spending money on expensive treatments later for ailments that you could have avoided altogether.

Throughout this book, all of the recipes were tested using organic produce, pasture-raised or grass-fed meats and poultry, wild-caught fish and shellfish, and farm-fresh eggs. Unsalted butter, extra virgin olive oil, coconut oil, unsweetened milks, and unadulterated herbs and spices are also part and parcel of putting the recipes together. It is important that you use the same quality of all of your ingredients when cooking. If you don't have a local farmers' market, you will find that many of these high quality products are available at supermarkets, chain stores, and specialty food shops, as well as online.

The eggs (remember, these are nature's perfect food) used in all of these recipes were direct-from-the-farm, but I realize that this is not always possible. You should, however, be aware of the different terminology used in commercial egg distribution, since eggs are so important in the *Grain Brain* diet. Following is a little tutorial so you will know which eggs are the best to buy.

- **Organic eggs** designate the feed and land on which the hens were raised rather than how they were raised. The hens may be held in cages or in open space, but, in most instances, they are cage-free. USDA organic certification requires that the feed used must have been produced on land that has had no toxins, chemical fertilizers, or pesticides applied for a minimum of 3 years. The hens cannot receive any antibiotics, hormones, invasive drugs, growth aids, or vaccines and must be fed purely on organic, non-genetically engineered feed.

- **Free-range eggs** are those gathered from hens who have indoor quarters, but who are allowed free roam in the outdoors (though often in an enclosed or fenced area). There is no stipulation about feed or drug use in their maintenance.

- **Cage-free eggs** simply imply that the hens are not raised in cages, but in some type of floor arrangement with nest crates in which they can lay their eggs. Again, there is no stipulation about feed or drug use in their maintenance.

Before you learn what foods you can have in your pantry, you'll have to sweep your kitchen clean of any items not allowed when cooking for your *Grain Brain* diet. The following list is long, so get some big boxes and pack up all of these banned foods and food products:

Grains and starches: Barley, bulghur, couscous, farina, graham flour, kamut, matzo meal, rye, semolina, spelt, triticale, wheat, wheat germ

General foods: Agave, canned baked beans, baked pastries and other baked goods, beer, blue cheeses, commercially prepared stocks, breads (including all whole grain and wholemeal types), all breaded food items, cakes, candy, cereals, commercially prepared chocolate milk, chutneys, cold cuts, communion wafers, cookies, cooking oils (soybean, corn, cottonseed, rapeseed, groundnut, safflower, grape seed, sunflower, rice bran, and wheat germ even if labeled organic), corn, crackers, crisps, doughnuts, dried fruits, egg substitutes, energy bars, flavored coffees and teas, commercially prepared or frozen French fries, fried vegetables and other foods, frozen yogurt, fruit fillings, golden syrup, gravies, honey, hot dogs, ice cream, all imitation meats and fish (such as surimi {fake crab meat}), instant hot drinks, jams (and jellies and preserves), juices, ketchup, malt/malt flavorings, malt vinegar, maple syrup, margarine, marinades, mayonnaise, meatballs and meatloaf prepared with breadcrumbs, muffins, non-dairy creamer, noodles, oats and oat bran (unless certified gluten-free), pasta, pizza dough, pizzas, potatoes, processed cheeses (such as Velveeta) and cheese spreads, puddings, roasted nuts, root beer, salad dressings, sausage, seitan, sherbets, soft drinks (sodas), soups, soy sauce, sports (and energy) drinks, sugar (all types), sugar-based snacks, syrups, tempura, teriyaki flavorings, trail mix, vegetable shortening, veggie burgers, vodka, wheatgrass, wine coolers, yams

Avoid all packaged foods labeled "fat-free" or "low-fat" unless they are authentically "fat-free" or "low-fat," such as vinegars, mustards, water, etc.

Avoid all unfermented soy (such as tofu, bean curd, and soy milk) and processed foods made with soy. Always check for "soy protein isolate" in the list of ingredients in any processed food. Eliminate all soy burgers, soy cheese, soy hot dogs, soy nuggets, soy ice cream, and soy milk yogurt. Although some naturally-brewed soy sauces are technically gluten-free, many commercial brands have trace amounts of gluten.

Ingredients in a packaged product that are often code for gluten: Amino peptide complex, Avena sativa, brown rice syrup, caramel color (frequently made from barley), cyclodextrin, dextrin, fermented grain extract, Hordeum distichon, Hordeum vulgare, hydrolysate, hydrolyzed malt extract, hydrolyzed vegetable protein, maltodextrin, modified food starch, natural flavoring, phytosphingosine extract, Secale cereal, soy protein, Triticum aestivum, Triticum vulgare, vegetable protein (HVP), yeast extract

Now that your kitchen is low-carb and gluten-free, you can restock with products that will make cooking a brain-healthy diet a cinch. When shopping, take care when eyeing those products labeled and marketed as "gluten-free," "low-carb," "sugar-free," and all of the other "frees" and health claims. Some of these foods might be just fine if they did not contain gluten or a high dosage of carbohydrates to begin with. But generally these labels come about because the foods have been highly processed, and one unhealthy ingredient has been replaced with another that is equally worrisome. In addition, trace amounts of gluten or sugars may remain in the processed item. Some of those so labeled might be breads, flours, desserts, prepared mixes, and so forth, which makes it very important for the consumer to be extremely well-informed, as well as prepared to carefully read labels of all items labeled in this fashion. Note: Although the FDA issued a regulation in August of 2013 to define the term "gluten free" (and variations like "free of gluten," and "no gluten") for food labeling, it still leaves the burden on the manufacturers to comply and be accountable for using the claim truthfully. The gluten limit for foods that carry any gluten-free label is less than 20 parts per million.

Now you are ready to shop.

The following items can be consumed liberally on your *Grain Brain* diet. To repeat: the preference is always fresh, local, and organic, but *individually quick frozen* or IQF organic foods can also be used. IQF foods are those that have been flash-frozen in individual pieces, such as a single prawn or blueberry, thereby preventing the frozen items from massing together and forming a solid block of icy food; but for your use, they should ideally be organically-grown.

Healthy oils and fats

- Extra virgin olive oil
- Coconut oil
- Walnut oil
- Avocado oil
- Organic or pasture-fed butter
- Ghee
- Almond butter
- Cashew butter
- Sesame seed butter (tahini)
- Grass-fed beef dripping

Raw or cured fruit fats

- Avocado
- Coconut
- Olives

25

"Milks"

- Unsweetened almond milk
- Unsweetened coconut milk

Nuts

- All raw or toasted nuts, except peanuts, which are a legume

(Note: When buying commercially packaged roasted nuts, check the label as they might have been processed with sugars or oils that should be avoided.)

Dairy products

- All cheeses except blue or highly processed (such as spreads and slices) cheeses

Seeds

- Flaxseed
- Chia seeds
- Sunflower seeds
- Pumpkin seeds
- Sesame seeds

Herbs, seasonings, and condiments

- All fresh and/or dried herbs, spices, and rhizomes

Many commercially-packed condiments and seasonings, such as mustard, horseradish, salsas, tapenades, vinegars, herb and spice mixes can be used IF they were made without the addition of wheat-derived vinegars or any sweetener other than natural stevia. Be aware that some packaged products are made at plants that process wheat and/or soy and may be contaminated.

Vegetables

- Alfalfa sprouts
- Artichokes
- Asparagus
- Beetroot
- Broccoli
- Broccoli rabe
- Brussels sprouts
- Cabbage – all types

- Cauliflower
- Celery
- Fennel
- Garlic
- Green beans
- Jicama
- Kale – all varieties
- Kohlrabi
- Leafy lettuces and greens
- Leeks
- Mushrooms – all types
- Onions – all types
- Pak choi
- Parsley
- Plantains
- Radishes – all types
- Sauerkraut
- Shallots
- Spinach
- Spring onions
- Swede
- Swiss chard – all types
- Turnips
- Water chestnuts
- Watercress

Low-sugar fruits Those with an asterisk (*) are substantially higher in sugar so be extra cautious about consuming these in moderation. There's nothing wrong with adding a fresh grapefruit to your breakfast, but you wouldn't want to then eat peaches and pears or other high-sugar fruits that day.

- Aubergine
- Avocado
- Cucumber
- Grapefruit*
- Kiwi*
- Lemons
- Limes
- Nectarines*
- Orange zest
- Peaches*
- Pears*
- Peppers – all colors
- Plums*
- Pumpkin
- Squash blossoms
- Squashes
- Tomatoes – all types
- Commercially-packed pickles IF no wheat-derived vinegar or sweetener used – check the label

Proteins

- Whole eggs
- Wild fish
  Cod
  Grouper
  Halibut
  Herring
  Mahi mahi
  Red snapper
  Salmon
  Sardines
  Sea bass
  Trout

- Shellfish and mollusks
  Calamari (squid)
  Clams
  Crab
  Lobster
  Mussels
  Octopus
  Oysters
  Prawns

- Grass-fed or pasture-raised-only meats
  Beef
  Bison
  Lamb
  Pork
  Veal

- Grass-fed organic meats
  Brain
  Heart
  Liver
  Kidneys
  Sweetbreads
  Tongue

- Free-range, organic poultry and wild birds
  Chicken
  Duck
  Goose
  Guinea fowl
  Ostrich
  Quail
  Turkey

The following foods can be used in moderation: Moderation means that you may eat small amounts (no more than 1 serving) of these ingredients once a day. Again, if you follow the recipes in this book, you'll learn how to smartly consume these ingredients. I don't intend for you to have to count carbs or weigh your food. The general principles outlined in this book will teach you how to make this new way of life effortless.

Non-gluten grains

- Amaranth
- Buckwheat
- Millet
- Oats (Note: Although oats do not naturally contain gluten, if they are processed at mills that also handle wheat they are frequently contaminated. Avoid them unless they come with a guarantee that they are gluten-free).
- Quinoa
- Rice (brown, white, wild)
- Sorghum
- Teff

Non-gluten flours used in very small amounts for dusting, coating, or thickening sauces only

- Tapioca starch
- Chestnut flour
- Brown rice flour

Legumes

- Dried beans
- Lentils
- Dried peas

Vegetables

- Carrots
- Parsnips

Dairy products (Use all very sparingly in recipes or as a topping)

- Cottage cheese
- Cow's milk and cream
- Kefir
- Yogurt

Whole sweet fruits

- Apples
- Apricots
- Bananas
- Berries (best choice)
- Cherries
- Grapes
- Mangoes
- Melons
- Papaya
- Pineapple
- Pomegranate

Note: Be extra cautious of sugary fruits such as apricots, mangoes, melons, papaya, and pineapple.

Sweeteners

- Natural stevia
- Dark chocolate having at least 70 percent or more cocoa content

Flavorings

- Cocoa powder

Alcohol

- Wine, preferably red if desired, but no more than one glass a day

BASICS

These are just a few recipes that will help you create terrific meals that meet the *Grain Brain* regimen. The most important ones are homemade stocks (both chicken and beef) and mayonnaise simply because they are used so often. A superb homemade stock pulled from the freezer can quickly turn into a satisfying lunch with the addition of some chopped greens and/or other vegetables, or a dinner with meat or cheese added. The sauces are clever multitaskers that can add zest to egg, vegetable, and meat dishes. There are a few other basics that I suggest that you have on hand at all times, and I've included recipes for these, too.

Basic Stock Making
Basic Vinaigrette
Balsamic Vinaigrette
Italian Vinaigrette
Spiced Vinaigrette
Tomato Sauce
Mayonnaise
Easy Hollandaise Sauce
Chimichurri
Tapenade
Creole Crunch

BASIC STOCK MAKING

Stocks are fundamental kitchen staples, and a homemade stock is ideal. For the *Grain Brain* regimen they are even more essential because many commercially prepared stocks or broths are laden with unnecessary ingredients and can be high in salt. When you make stock yourself, you have control over the ingredients, the seasoning, and the outcome. Broths can be used in place of stocks although they tend to be richer as they are usually made with meat, rather than bones.

For a rich stock, roast the bones (chicken, veal, or beef) and, if you want really rich stock, add pieces of fresh meat to the roasting bones. Bones that are not roasted will result in a light stock, both in color and flavor.

1.8 kg (4 lb) chicken, beef, or veal bones

1 carrot, peeled and chopped

1 rib celery, chopped

1 small onion, peeled and chopped

6 peppercorns

5 sprigs flat-leaf parsley

2 bay leaves

Place the bones in a large stockpot and cover with cold water by at least 5 cm (2 inches). This amount of cold water ensures that the collagen (the gelatin-forming agent) is extracted from the bones as the liquid heats. Adding the bones to hot water would seal them, keeping the collagen inside, and since much of the flavor comes from the collagen and cartilage, you don't want to lose any of the deliciousness. Do not add salt to the water. Salt can be added when you use the stock in a recipe. Bring to a boil.

Add the carrot, celery, onion, peppercorns, parsley, and bay leaves. Be sure to skim off the scum that rises to the top. Again, bring to a boil, lower the heat and cook, skimming frequently, at a bare simmer for about 1 hour or until the stock is very flavorful.

Remove from the heat and pour through a fine mesh strainer. If you want very clear stock, put a double layer of muslin in the strainer before pouring.

Place the strained stock in a clean container in a large bowl of ice to chill quickly. As it chills, the fat will rise to the top along with some impurities which can be skimmed off.

When cool, pour the stock into small (perhaps 250-ml/8-fl oz) containers for ease of use, and store, covered and refrigerated, for up to 2 days or frozen for up to 3 months.

If you don't want to make stock, buy the best quality canned low-sodium organic chicken or beef stock or broth you can find. Keep a supply of canned stock or broth in the pantry for last-minute kitchen emergencies.

Beef Stock Nutritional Analysis per Serving (250 ml/8 fl oz): calories 15, carbohydrates 1 g, fiber 3 g, protein 4 g, fat 0 g, sodium 75 mg, sugar 1 g.

Chicken Stock Nutritional Analysis per Serving (250 ml/8 fl oz): calories 10, carbohydrates 1 g, fiber 0 g, protein 2 g, fat 0 g, sodium 65 mg, sugar 0 g.

BASIC VINAIGRETTE

Makes about 500 ml (17 fl oz)

This vinaigrette keeps well, covered and refrigerated. Not only is it a quick salad dressing, but it also adds flavor when drizzled on grilled fish, shellfish, pork, or poultry.

375 ml (13 fl oz) extra virgin olive oil

6 tablespoons red or white wine vinegar

Salt and pepper

Combine the oil, vinegar, salt, and pepper in a resealable container - a glass jar with a lid works well. Cover and shake vigorously to emulsify.

Use immediately or cover and store, at room temperature, for up to 3 days or refrigerated for up to 1 month. If refrigerated, bring to room temperature and shake to blend before using.

VARIATIONS You can add 1 small finely chopped shallot and/or 1 table-spoon of finely chopped flat-leaf parsley or chives to the basic recipe.

Nutritional Analysis per Serving (1 tablespoon): calories 90, carbohydrates 0 g, fiber 0 g, protein 0 g, fat 11 g, sodium 37 mg, sugar 0 g.

BALSAMIC VINAIGRETTE

Makes 500 ml (17 fl oz)

This is one of the most useful vinaigrettes to have as a pantry staple. It is a perfect drizzle for grilled vegetables, meats, poultry, or meaty fish as well as a delicious salad topper.

375 ml (13 fl oz) extra virgin olive oil
125 ml (4 fl oz) balsamic vinegar
1 teaspoon Dijon mustard
Salt and pepper

Combine the oil, vinegar, mustard, salt, and pepper in a resealable container – a glass jar with a lid works well. Cover and shake vigorously to emulsify.

Use immediately or cover and store, at room temperature, for up to 3 days or refrigerated for up to 1 month. If refrigerated, bring to room temperature and shake to blend before using.

VARIATIONS You can add 1 small finely chopped shallot and/or 1 tablespoon of finely chopped basil, flat-leaf parsley, or chives to the basic recipe.

Nutritional Analysis per Serving (1 tablespoon): calories 92, carbohydrates 1 g, fiber 0 g, protein 0 g, fat 11 g, sodium 41 mg, sugar 18 g.

ITALIAN VINAIGRETTE

Makes 250 ml (8 fl oz)

If you use fresh herbs for this dressing, it won't be traditionally Italian because true Italian cooks prefer dried. Fresh herbs also offer an entirely different flavor than dried. The ratio of oil to vinegar is different than in a classic French vinaigrette and makes the mix quite acidic. This recipe works best on salads with firm lettuces or those that predominantly feature vegetables. Italian Vinaigrette also makes a wonderful marinade for steaks or chops.

125 ml (4 fl oz) red wine vinegar

1 teaspoon finely chopped garlic

1 teaspoon dried oregano

1 teaspoon dried parsley

250 ml (8 fl oz) extra virgin olive oil

Salt and pepper

Combine the vinegar, garlic, oregano, and parsley in a resealable container – a glass jar with a lid works well. Add the olive oil along with salt and pepper, cover, and shake vigorously to emulsify.

Use immediately or cover and store, at room temperature, for up to 3 days or refrigerated for up to 1 week. If refrigerated, bring to room temperature and shake to blend before using.

Nutritional Analysis per Serving (1 tablespoon): calories 121, carbohydrates 0 g, fiber 0 g, protein 0 g, fat 14 g, sodium 75 mg, sugar 0 g.

SPICED VINAIGRETTE

Makes about 325 ml (11 fl oz)

The toasted spice in this vinaigrette makes it a wonderful drizzle for grilled meats or fish as well as an aromatic dressing for vegetable salads.

Although it calls for toasted cumin, you can use curry powder, Aleppo pepper or paprika, or any spice you like, except sweet spices like cinnamon. If you are using seeds, it is always best to toast them and then grind them into a powder in a spice grinder. However, even pre-ground spices and spice mixes are enhanced by toasting.

250 ml (8 fl oz) extra virgin olive oil

75 ml (3 fl oz) lemon juice

2 tablespoons freshly ground toasted cumin (about 1½ tablespoons seeds)

Salt and pepper

Combine the oil, lemon juice, and cumin in a resealable container – a glass jar with a lid works well. Season with salt and pepper to taste, cover, and shake vigorously to emulsify.

Use immediately or cover and store, at room temperature, for up to 3 days or refrigerated for up to 1 week. If refrigerated, bring to room temperature and shake to blend before using.

Nutritional Analysis per Serving (1 tablespoon): calories 93, carbohydrates 1 g, fiber 0 g, protein 0 g, fat 11 g, sodium 55 mg, sugar 0 g.

TOMATO SAUCE

Makes about 1.5 liters (2½ pints)

This is a basic tomato sauce that can be used as a component of casseroles or gratins or as the base for a more flavorful sauce when herbs, spices, vegetables, and/or meats are added. Of course, in the height of summer when tomatoes are at their most delicious, by all means make this sauce with fresh-off-the-vine ones.

4 x 400-g (14-oz) cans chopped plum tomatoes with their juice

250 ml (8 fl oz) passata

60 g (2 oz) unsalted butter

Salt and pepper

Combine the tomatoes and the passata in a heavy-bottom saucepan over low heat. When hot, begin adding the butter in small amounts until it blends into the sauce. Season with salt and pepper to taste and continue to cook on low until the sauce has thickened slightly. It is hard to give an exact time as it will depend upon the liquid in the tomatoes and the looseness of the passata, but it should be no more than about 30 minutes.

Remove from the heat and cool. Store, covered and refrigerated, for up to 1 week or frozen for up to 3 months. If freezing, it is a good idea to do so in 250-ml (8-fl oz) containers for ease of use.

Nutritional Analysis per Serving (125 ml/4 fl oz): calories 65, carbohydrates 7 g, fiber 2 g, protein 2 g, fat 4 g, sodium 283 mg, sugar 5 g.

MAYONNAISE

Makes about 500 ml (17 fl oz)

Although jarred mayonnaise is in almost everybody's refrigerator, it is so simple to make and tastes so good that I recommend you make your own. This gives you the assurance that it is both gluten- and carbohydrate-free. You can make mayonnaise by hand using a whisk, but the blender method is quicker and easier on your wrist.

3 large egg yolks, at room temperature (see Note)

½ teaspoon salt

¼ teaspoon dry mustard powder

1 tablespoon champagne vinegar or lemon juice

375–500 ml (13–17 fl oz) extra virgin olive oil or avocado oil

About 1 tablespoon hot water

Fill the blender jar with boiling water and set it aside for a couple of minutes. You just need to heat the jar to help the eggs thicken.

Pour out the water and quickly wipe the jar dry.

Place the jar on the motor. Add the egg yolks and process on medium until very thick. Add the salt and mustard and quickly incorporate. Add the vinegar and process to blend.

With the motor running, begin pouring in the oil at an excruciatingly slow drip. The slower the drip, the more even the emulsification. When about half of the oil has been added you should have a sauce that is like thick cream, and you can begin adding the oil just a bit quicker as curdling will no longer be an issue. If the mixture seems too thick after you have added all of the oil – you want a soft, creamy consistency – add just a smidge more vinegar or just enough hot water to smooth the mix.

Scrape the mayonnaise into a clean container with a lid. Cover and refrigerate for up to 5 days.

VARIATIONS To the above recipe, you can add 2 tablespoons chopped fresh herbs, or finely chopped green or red hot chillies, grated ginger root, grated horseradish, or finely chopped sweet peppers to taste. Ground spices can also vary the flavor; cumin, cayenne, and cracked black pepper are favorite additions.

NOTE Although we have heard concerns about eating uncooked eggs, if you use high-quality eggs that have been properly stored along with the quantity of acid called for in this recipe, there should be no risk. However, homemade mayonnaise does not keep, even covered and refrigerated, for long periods of time. It is best consumed when made.

Nutritional Analysis per Serving (1 tablespoon): calories 95, carbohydrates 0 g, fiber 0 g, protein 0 g, fat 11 g, sodium 37 mg, sugar 0 g.

EASY HOLLANDAISE SAUCE

Makes about 175 ml (6 fl oz)

Blender hollandaise was introduced, I believe, by Julia Child in the late 1960s. It made home cooks much more willing to try recipes calling for hollandaise as the classic method takes skill and patience. Although best known as the sauce for Eggs Benedict, it can turn a dish of steamed vegetables into an elegant and satisfying meal.

3 large egg yolks, at room temperature

1 tablespoon lemon juice, strained

$^3/_4$ teaspoon salt or to taste

$^1/_2$ teaspoon Tabasco sauce or to taste

125 ml (4 fl oz) hot clarified unsalted butter (see Note)

Place the egg yolks, lemon juice, salt and Tabasco in a blender and process on medium speed for 45 seconds. With the blender running, add the hot clarified butter in a very slow, steady stream and process until the mixture is very smooth and slightly thickened.

Scrape the sauce from the blender into the top half of a double boiler placed over very hot water, and keep warm until ready to use.

NOTE Clarified butter is the clear liquid that appears when the butterfat separates from the water and milk solids in slowly melted butter. To make clarified butter, cut 450 g (1 lb) unsalted butter into cubes and place it in a medium saucepan over *very low* heat. Cook, without stirring and without the butter bubbling and/or browning, for 20 minutes. Strain the yellow liquid that rises to the top into a clean container, discarding all of the solids. Cool to room temperature; then cover and refrigerate for up to 1 week or freeze for up to 6 months. Reheat the clarified butter as needed.

South Asian style clarified butter is called ghee. It is made in much the same way as plain clarified butter, but it often has additives, such as spices or herbs. Its quality depends upon the butter used and the length of time that it is cooked.

Nutritional Analysis per Serving (3 tablespoons): calories 294, carbohydrates 1 g, fiber 0 g, protein 2 g, fat 31 g, sodium 445 mg, sugar 0 g.

CHIMICHURRI

Makes about 375 ml (13 fl oz)

This is my version of a classic Argentinean meat condiment. Although wonderful on steaks, it can be used on almost anything, from seafood to meat to vegetables, to add a delightfully fresh flavor. It should be made no more than a couple of hours before using so that the herbs retain their bright color and taste. It is one of the most refreshing sauces I know.

50 g (1³/₄ oz) flat-leaf parsley leaves, chopped

50 g (1³/₄ oz) spring onions, green and white part, chopped

2 tablespoons chopped oregano

2 tablespoons chopped coriander leaves

1 tablespoon finely chopped garlic

Juice and freshly grated zest of 1 lemon

250 ml (8 fl oz) extra virgin olive oil

3 tablespoons white wine vinegar

Salt and pepper

Combine the parsley, spring onions, oregano, coriander, garlic, and lemon zest in the bowl of a food processor fitted with a metal blade. Add the lemon juice and process, using quick on and off turns, to just finely chopped.

Scrape the mixture from the processor bowl into a clean container. Add the oil and vinegar, stirring to blend. Season with salt and pepper and serve.

Chimichurri can be stored, covered, and refrigerated for a day. Note that the longer you store the darker the color, and you want it to be a fresh green.

Nutritional Analysis per Serving (1 tablespoon): calories 168, carbohydrates 2 g, fiber 1 g, protein 1 g, fat 19 g, sodium 103 mg, sugar 0 g.

TAPENADE

Makes 500 ml (17 fl oz)

This pungent mix is a typical Provençal dish that in France is generally served on small toasts along with an aperitif. I find it works marvels with raw or lightly steamed vegetables. It can also be used to stuff poultry or pork. Tapenade traditionally has anchovies, but I've made them optional here. Sometimes we make a couple of batches – one with anchovies and one without – simply because, either way, it is such a tasty dip.

6 tablespoons extra virgin olive oil

2 tablespoons finely chopped onion

1 tablespoon finely chopped garlic

75 g (2³/₄ oz) red pepper, chopped

75 g (2³/₄ oz) yellow pepper, chopped

75 g (2³/₄ oz) green pepper, chopped

190 g (6³/₄ oz) black olives, chopped

85 g (3 oz) walnuts, chopped

3 tablespoons chopped flat-leaf parsley

1 tablespoon finely chopped basil

1 tablespoon well-drained chopped capers

4 tablespoons red wine vinegar

1 x 55-g (2-oz) can anchovies, chopped, optional

Salt and pepper

Heat the oil in a heavy-bottom saucepan over medium heat. Add the onion and garlic and cook, stirring, for about 3 minutes or just until they begin to color. Add the red, yellow, and green pepper and cook, stirring occasionally, for an additional 6 minutes or just until the peppers have softened.

Stir in the olives, walnuts, parsley, basil, and capers. When blended, add the vinegar, anchovies, if using, and salt and pepper to taste. Lower the heat and cook for 5 minutes or until the flavors have blended and the mixture is slightly thick.

Remove from the heat and set aside to cool. Use immediately or store, covered and refrigerated, for up to 3 weeks.

Nutritional Analysis per Serving (2 tablespoons): calories 52, carbohydrates 1 g, fiber 0 g, protein 1 g, fat 5 g, sodium 113 mg, sugar 0 g.

CREOLE CRUNCH

Makes about 600 ml (1 pint)

Creole flavors combine French, African, and Spanish influences to make them extremely zesty. A bit more refined than Cajun, this crunchy rub adds a bit of spice and a heat to pork, chicken, steaks, and burgers as well as to prawns and fish. If you like heat, add cayenne pepper to taste.

60 g (2 oz) dried onion flakes

25 g (1 oz) sweet red pepper flakes

3 tablespoons hot paprika

3 tablespoons dried thyme

3 tablespoons dried oregano

3 tablespoons pepper

2 tablespoons cayenne pepper or to taste

2 tablespoons celery seeds

1 tablespoon garlic granules

Combine all of the ingredients in a small bowl, mixing to blend well. Transfer to an airtight container and store in a cool, dry spot for up to 6 months.

Nutritional Analysis per Serving (1 tablespoon): calories 13, carbohydrates 3 g, fiber 1 g, protein 1 g, fat 0 g, sodium 2 mg, sugar 1 g.

BREAKFAST

I have found that breakfast is one of the most difficult meals to adjust for people new to the *Grain Brain* diet. This is mostly because so many have, for years, begun their day with a hot drink and some type of bread, without any thought to proper nutrition. The hale and hearty farm breakfast of America's early years simply doesn't exist anymore and, even if it did, it would probably now contain foods high in gluten and carbohydrates that, I believe, do not broadcast good health. Eggs and bacon have been so maligned that everyone has become afraid to consume them; I insist that eggs, nature's perfect food, be on the table, daily. The foods that start your day will set the right tone for the rest of your life.

I am going to give you some extraordinary alternatives to that cuppa and muffin that you have been grabbing and eating on the go. At the *Grain Brain* breakfast table, nuts, eggs, seeds, vegetables, and meat are now going to be part of every morning's start.

Morning Wake-Up Call
Rise and Shine Shake
Quick Crunchy *"Grain Brain"* Cereal
Ungranola
Homemade Turkey Sausage
Grain Brain Breakfast Hash
Eggs Benedict

Courgette Pancakes

Roasted Onion Omelette with Sun-Dried Tomato and Onion Chutney

Manchego Tortilla

Torta Rustica

MORNING WAKE-UP CALL

Serves 1

There's no better way to start the day than with an energy boost. Quick to prepare, smooth to drink, and filled with goodness; this creamy green juice brightens the morning rush. The juice is smoother when processed in a juicer but works just fine in a blender, also. It is particularly important that you use organically grown, well-washed ingredients.

    8 large leaves kale
    4 ribs celery
    1 cucumber
    2.5-cm (1-inch) piece ginger root
    1 avocado, peeled, pitted, and chopped
    ½ lemon, seeds removed

Place all of the ingredients in an electric juicer and process to juice. Alternatively, chop the kale, celery, cucumber, and ginger and place them in a blender. Add the avocado and the juice of the ½ lemon and process on high until smooth.

Drink immediately.

Nutritional Analysis per Serving: calories 652, carbohydrates 77 g, fiber 29 g, protein 30 g, fat 35 g, sodium 352 mg, sugar 9 g.

RISE AND SHINE SHAKE

Serves 1

This shake is a fabulous wake-up in a glass. You can change the flavor and the health benefits if you like by replacing the blueberries with half of an avocado and the almond milk with unsweetened coconut milk. Either way, it's a delicious, nutritious shake.

55 g (2 oz) frozen blueberries

4 tablespoons almond meal/flour or freshly pulverized almonds

2 tablespoons ground flaxseed

2 tablespoons almond butter

375 ml (13 fl oz) ice-cold unsweetened almond milk

Combine the blueberries, almond meal, flaxseed, and almond butter in a blender jar. Add the milk along with a couple of ice cubes and process until it reaches a shake-like consistency. If too thick, add cold water or additional almond milk.

Nutritional Analysis per Serving: calories 502, carbohydrates 26 g, fiber 12 g, protein 17 g, fat 41 g, sodium 218 mg, sugar 9 g.

QUICK CRUNCHY *"GRAIN BRAIN"* CEREAL

Serves 1

This recipe is in my book *Grain Brain*, but I thought it should be included here, too, as it meets all of my dietary guidelines and is so straightforward to put together for a quick and healthy breakfast. You can use any raw, unsalted nut that you like.

75 g (2³/₄ oz) raw, unsalted walnuts, crushed

4 tablespoons unsweetened coconut flakes

1 handful (about 55 g/2 oz) fresh organic berries

150 ml (¹/₄ pint) unsweetened almond milk or whole-fat milk

Combine the walnuts, coconut flakes, and berries in a cereal bowl. Add the milk and stir to combine.

Nutritional Analysis per Serving: calories 518, carbohydrates 20 g, fiber 8 g, protein 10 g, fat 47 g, sodium 127 mg, sugar 8 g.

UNGRANOLA

Makes about 450 g (1 lb)

This mimics granola, but without any grain added to it this quasi-cereal completely meets the *Grain Brain* breakfast rules. If you don't have ghee or clarified butter on hand, coconut oil or extra virgin olive oil will work just fine. Watch carefully as you bake, as the nuts can quickly turn from golden and toasty to dark and inedible. If you grow to love this mix, double or triple the recipe and keep it on hand for snacking as well as a wholesome start to your day.

150 g (5¼ oz) unblanched almonds, chopped

150 g (5¼ oz) raw cashews, chopped

100 g (3½ oz) raw pumpkin seeds

60 g (2 oz) unsweetened coconut flakes, chopped

2 tablespoons flaxseed

1 tablespoon chia seeds

1 teaspoon ground cinnamon

½ teaspoon ground nutmeg

½ teaspoon ground allspice

1 tablespoon stevia

3 tablespoons clarified butter (see page 40) or ghee

Preheat the oven to 180ºC/350ºF/Gas Mark 4.

Line a baking sheet with parchment paper or a nonstick silicone pan liner. Set aside.

Combine the almonds, cashews, pumpkin seeds, coconut flakes, flaxseed, chia seeds, cinnamon, nutmeg, and allspice in a mixing bowl. Stir in the stevia. When well blended, drizzle with butter or oil and toss to coat.

Pour the mixture onto the baking sheet and, using a spatula, spread it out to an even layer. Place in the preheated oven and bake, stirring occasionally, for about 25 minutes or until nicely toasted and aromatic.

Remove from the oven and place the baking sheet on a wire rack to allow the mixture to cool. When cool, store in a covered container in a cool spot for up to 3 days or refrigerate for up to 1 month.

Nutritional Analysis per Serving (55 g/2 oz): calories 457, carbohydrates 15 g, fiber 6 g, protein 13 g, fat 40 g, sodium 11 mg, sugar 3 g.

HOMEMADE TURKEY SAUSAGE

Makes 6 patties

We don't usually think about making our own breakfast sausage, but we should. It's a cinch to make and can be stored for future use in dishes. The mix also makes a wonderful addition to frittatas and quiches, but for the morning rush, I simply fry up a patty along with a couple of scrambled eggs seasoned with chopped spring onions and I'm good to go.

2 tablespoons extra virgin olive oil

225 g (8 oz) onions, peeled and finely chopped

1 tablespoon finely chopped garlic

Salt and pepper

1½ teaspoons chopped sage

1 teaspoon chopped thyme

1 teaspoon chopped flat-leaf parsley

½ teaspoon ground allspice

Cayenne pepper

565 g (1 lb 4 oz) minced turkey

Heat the olive oil in a medium frying pan over medium heat. Add the onion and garlic, season with salt and pepper to taste, and cook, stirring frequently, for about 5 minutes or until very soft and just beginning to color. Stir in the sage, thyme, parsley, allspice, and cayenne pepper to taste and continue to cook for another minute. Remove from the heat and set aside to cool.

When the aromatics are cool, place the turkey in a mixing bowl. Add the cooled onion mixture and stir to blend completely.

To taste for proper seasoning, form a tiny amount of the mixture into a patty and fry it in a bit of olive oil over medium heat until just cooked through. Taste and, if necessary, season the raw mix with additional salt, pepper, herbs, and/or cayenne.

Using your hands, form the raw mixture into 6 patties of equal size. They may be refrigerated, separated by a small sheet of grease-proof paper, in a resealable plastic bag for up to 2 days, frozen for up to 3 months, or cooked immediately.

When ready to cook, heat a slight slick of olive oil in a nonstick frying pan over medium heat. Add the patties and fry, turning occasionally, for about 10 minutes, until cooked through and brown or until an instant-read thermometer reads 74ºC/165ºF when inserted into the thickest section.

Nutritional Analysis per Serving (1 patty): calories 255, carbohydrates 3 g, fiber 1 g, protein 26 g, fat 16 g, sodium 183 mg, sugar 1 g.

GRAIN BRAIN BREAKFAST HASH

Serves 6

This is my version of an old-fashioned New England "red flannel" hash. It is usually made with corned beef and potatoes, but I think this version is even better than the classic. Traditionally, the hash should be topped with a poached or fried egg. If you choose to add the egg, bake the hash in individual dishes (ramekins will do nicely) and then top each serving with an egg and a sprinkle of chopped parsley. You would then have a sensational brunch dish.

2 tablespoons extra virgin olive oil

225 g (8 oz) onions, finely diced

1 tablespoon finely chopped garlic

Salt and pepper

1 large beetroot, roasted, peeled, and finely diced

150 g (5¼ oz) raw kale, finely chopped

450 g (1 lb) cooked roast beef, finely diced

1 teaspoon gluten-free Worcestershire sauce, optional

4 tablespoons grated Parmesan cheese

Preheat the oven to 190ºC/375ºF/Gas Mark 5.

Heat the oil in a large, ovenproof frying pan over medium heat. Add the onion and garlic, season with salt and pepper to taste, and cook, stirring frequently, for about 5 minutes or until very soft and just beginning to color.

Stir in the beetroot and kale and continue to cook for another minute or two or just until the kale has wilted. Add the beef along with the Worcestershire sauce and stir to blend completely. Taste and, if necessary, adjust the seasoning.

Pat the mixture down to an even layer and sprinkle the top with the cheese. Transfer to the preheated oven and bake for about 20 minutes or until the top is golden brown and crisp.

Remove from the oven and serve.

Nutritional Analysis per Serving: calories 261, carbohydrates 7 g, fiber 1 g, protein 24 g, fat 15 g, sodium 239 mg, sugar 2 g.

EGGS BENEDICT

Serves 4

How can you have Eggs Benedict without the traditional English muffin you might ask? Well, you just ditch the muffin and place the ham and eggs on a crispy courgette pancake. A little more work for the cook, but extra pleasure for the diner. I always make more pancakes than I need because people invariably ask for another. I assure you that you'll never go back to that muffin. Of course, if you are short on time, the eggs and sauce can be placed on a bed of leafy greens.

For perfect Eggs Benedict, featuring eggs with tender whites and runny yolks, you must gently poach the eggs in just barely simmering water. They should never be cooked at a hard simmer or boil or the whites will become tough and the yolks firm. Since there is now much concern about the safety of lightly cooked eggs, I barely poach the eggs and then hold them in a saucepan of very warm water (55ºC/130°F) for 15 minutes. This method allows the cook to prepare the remaining ingredients as the eggs warm and cook.

1 tablespoon white vinegar

4 extra large eggs, at room temperature

4 slices back bacon

4 Courgette Pancakes (recipe follows)

1 recipe Hollandaise Sauce (see page 40)

1 tablespoon chopped flat-leaf parsley

Preheat the oven to 140ºC/275°F/Gas Mark 1.

Heat about 7.5 cm (3 inches) of water in a large shallow pan over medium heat until bubbles form around the edge. Add the vinegar.

In another pan of similar size, heat 7.5 cm (3 inches) of water to 55ºC/130°F on a sugar thermometer. Remove from the heat and keep warm.

Working quickly with one egg at a time, carefully break each egg into a small cup and then gently slide the egg from the cup into the barely simmering vinegar-water. When all of the eggs have been added, cook for about 2 minutes or until the whites are just set but the yolks are still very loose.

Using a slotted spoon, carefully lift the barely cooked eggs, one at a time, and place them into the 55ºC/130°F water. Cover and let rest for 15 minutes. You should, from time to time, check the temperature of the water. If it falls below 55ºC/130°F, slowly add enough boiling water to bring the temperature back to the desired temperature.

Place the bacon in a large nonstick frying pan over medium-high heat. Fry, turning occasionally, for about 4 minutes or until just lightly browned around the edges. Remove from the heat and place on a baking sheet in the preheated oven to keep warm.

Place a warm pancake in the center of each plate and top with a slice of bacon. Using a slotted spoon, lift the poached eggs, one at a time, from the water and pat gently with clean kitchen paper to remove excess water. Place an egg on top of the bacon. (If the edges of the eggs are a bit ragged, carefully trim them with a small knife or with kitchen scissors.)

Spoon an equal portion (about 3 tablespoons) of the Hollandaise Sauce on top of each egg, sprinkle with chopped parsley, and serve immediately.

NOTE For those on a restricted sodium diet, the bacon can be eliminated from the recipe.

Nutritional Analysis per Serving (includes the courgette pancake and hollandaise sauce): calories 485, carbohydrates 6 g, fiber 1 g, protein 16 g, fat 44 g, sodium 858 mg, sugar 2 g.

COURGETTE PANCAKES

Makes about 8

3 large courgettes

1 extra large egg white

2 tablespoons almond meal

1 teaspoon paprika

Salt and pepper

3 tablespoons clarified butter (see page 40) or ghee

Using either a hand-held grater or a food processor fitted with the shredding blade, shred the courgettes.

When shredded, place the courgettes in the center of a large piece of clean kitchen paper. Bring the sides up and twist hard to express all of the liquid. You may have to do this a few times as the drier the courgettes, the crisper the pancakes will be.

Place the shredded, drained courgettes in a large mixing bowl. Add the egg white, almond meal, paprika, salt, and pepper, tossing to blend in the seasonings.

Heat the butter in a large frying pan over medium heat. When very hot, but not smoking, spoon in the courgette mixture to make individual circles about 9 cm (3½ inches) in diameter. Fry, turning once, for about 5 minutes or until cooked through, golden brown, and crisp.

Using a spatula, transfer to a double layer of kitchen paper to drain.

If necessary, place on a baking sheet in a low oven to keep warm until ready to serve.

Nutritional Analysis per Serving (1 pancake): calories 76, carbohydrates 3 g, fiber 1 g, protein 2 g, fat 6 g, sodium 90 mg, sugar 2 g.

ROASTED ONION OMELETTE WITH SUN-DRIED TOMATO AND ONION CHUTNEY

Serves 6

This is a sensational breakfast, brunch, lunch, or light supper omelette that can be served either hot or at room temperature. I always try to have some left over because it makes such a tasty addition to green salads for supper. The Indian spices are so aromatic that you need almost nothing else to create a memorable meal. The chutney can also be used as a condiment for grilled meats, poultry, or fish.

10 large eggs

4 tablespoons chopped coriander

1 teaspoon curry powder, preferably hot

1/2 teaspoon ground toasted cumin

Pinch ground turmeric

Pinch cayenne pepper or to taste

Salt and pepper

2 tablespoons extra virgin olive oil

340 g (12 oz) roasted, sliced onions (see Note)

1 teaspoon mashed roasted garlic (see Note)

1/2 teaspoon finely chopped ginger root

150 g (5¼ oz) leafy greens, such as kale or spring greens, finely
    chopped

200 g (7 oz) peeled and seeded plum tomatoes, well drained and
    finely diced

75 g (2¾ oz) mushrooms, cleaned and chopped

1 teaspoon finely chopped hot green chilli or to taste

Sun-Dried Tomato and Onion Chutney (recipe follows)

Break the eggs into a mixing bowl and whisk to blend. Add the
coriander, curry powder, cumin, turmeric, and cayenne and combine.
Season with salt and pepper to taste. Set aside.

Heat the oil in a large, nonstick sauté pan over medium heat. Add
the roasted onions, garlic, and ginger and sauté for 2 minutes. Stir in
the greens, tomatoes, mushrooms, and chilli and sauté for about 5
minutes or until the flavors have combined and the vegetables are
very hot.

Pour the seasoned eggs into the pan, lifting and twisting so that
the eggs cover the vegetables. Lower the heat and cover. Cook for
about 12 minutes or until the eggs are set and the bottom is brown.
You can turn the omelette if you wish to brown both sides but it is
not necessary. Alternatively, you can use an ovenproof frying pan and
bake the omelette.

Flip the cooked omelette onto a serving platter (preferably one that has been warmed). Cut into 6 wedges and serve immediately with Sun-Dried Tomato and Onion Chutney.

NOTE To make 340 g (12 oz) roasted onions, combine 900 g (2 lb) diced onions with 4 tablespoons olive oil and season with salt and pepper to taste. Spread out on a nonstick baking dish and place in a preheated 180°C/350°F/Gas Mark 4 oven. Roast, tossing occasionally, for about 30 minutes or until the onions are golden brown and most of the moisture has cooked out. Roasted onions may be added to other egg dishes or used as a flavoring accent for other vegetables or sauces.

To make roasted garlic: If roasting whole heads, lay the head on its side and using a sharp knife, cut about 3 mm ($1/8$ inch) off the stem end. Lightly coat the entire head(s) or cloves of garlic with olive oil. Wrap tightly in aluminium foil and place them in a baking dish in the preheated 180°C/350ºF/Gas Mark 4 oven. Roast until soft and aromatic: whole heads should take about 25 minutes and individual cloves about 12 minutes. Remove from the oven, unwrap, and let cool slightly.

Using your fingertips, push the flesh from the skin. The clove may or may not pop out whole, but either way it doesn't matter as roasted garlic usually gets mashed or puréed before use. May be used immediately or stored, covered and refrigerated, for up to 1 week.

Nutritional Analysis per Serving (including 1 tablespoon chutney): calories 325, carbohydrates 20 g, fiber 4 g, protein 14 g, fat 22 g, sodium 323 mg, sugar 8 g.

SUN-DRIED TOMATO AND ONION CHUTNEY

Makes about 750 ml (1¼ pints)

675 g (1 lb 8 oz) sweet onions, peeled and chopped
115 g (4 oz) sun-dried tomatoes (not packed in oil), chopped
2 tablespoons finely chopped ginger root

1 tablespoon finely chopped fresh hot red or green chilli

1 tablespoon stevia

1 tablespoon chilli powder

2 teaspoons mustard seeds

1 teaspoon cumin seeds

125 ml (4 fl oz) cider vinegar

1 tablespoon lemon juice

Combine the onions, tomatoes, ginger, and chilli in a heavy-bottom saucepan (preferably nonstick). Stir in the stevia and chilli powder along with the mustard and cumin seeds. Add the vinegar and lemon juice and stir to combine. Place over medium heat and cook, stirring frequently, for about 30 minutes or until the onions are very soft and the mixture is quite thick with well-balanced flavor. If the mixture gets too thick before the onions have softened, add water or tomato juice, 4 tablespoons at a time, to thin.

Remove from the heat and allow to come to room temperature. Store, covered and refrigerated, for up to 1 month.

Nutritional Analysis per Serving (1 tablespoon): calories 15, carbohydrates 3 g, fiber 1 g, protein 1 g, fat 0 g, sodium 4 mg, sugar 1 g.

MANCHEGO TORTILLA

Serves 6

No, no, no – this is not the tortilla you are thinking of. In Spain, an omelette is known as a tortilla and the traditional one (*tortilla de patatas*) contains potatoes, which I have eliminated to make this a *Grain Brain* favorite. Prepared in a pan especially made to create a soft, juicy finished cake about 30 cm (12 inches) across and 4 cm (1½ inches) deep, this classic Spanish dish can be found in tapas bars throughout Spain.

In making this tortilla, it is most important to prepare it in a good amount of spicy extra virgin olive oil (see Note) and in an ovenproof nonstick pan. For extra-special Spanish flavor, add about 340 g (12 oz) chopped free-range, organic chorizo when you are sautéing the leeks and garlic.

If you can't find Manchego cheese, you can substitute Asiago or a mature Cheddar.

75 ml (3 fl oz) spicy extra virgin olive oil

340 g (12 oz) leeks, chopped, white part only

1 teaspoon finely chopped garlic

Salt and pepper

340 g (12 oz) well-drained artichoke hearts (if frozen, thaw and
    drain very well), roughly chopped

8 large eggs

140 g (5 oz) chopped Manzanilla olives

175 g (6 oz) thinly sliced Manchego cheese

Preheat the oven to 180ºC/350ºF/Gas Mark 4.

Heat the olive oil in a 30-cm (12-inch) ovenproof, nonstick frying pan over medium heat. Add the leeks and garlic. Season with salt and pepper to taste and sauté for about 4 minutes or just until softened. Add the artichoke hearts and cook for an additional 2 minutes. Remove from the heat and, using the back of a spatula, pat the artichoke mixture evenly into the pan.

Combine the eggs and olives, beating to blend very well. Pour half of the egg mixture over the artichoke mixture; it should just barely cover. Lay about two-thirds of the cheese over the top and then pour the remaining egg mixture into the pan. Transfer to the preheated oven and bake for about 15 minutes or until well set and beginning to brown.

Remove from the oven and cover the top with the remaining cheese. Return to the oven and continue to bake for an additional 5 minutes or until the cheese has melted and browned.

Again, remove from the oven and place on a wire rack to rest for 5 minutes. Then, invert the tortilla onto a serving plate, cut into 6 wedges, and serve hot or at room temperature.

NOTE A green, acidic, spicy extra virgin olive oil can only be found by asking your shopkeeper which of the fine olive oils can be classified as such. Often, specialty markets or Italian food stores will have samples available for tasting which is, by far, the best way to find the olive oil that appeals to your palate.

Nutritional Analysis per Serving: calories 399, carbohydrates 15 g, fiber 8 g, protein 18 g, fat 31 g, sodium 658 mg, sugar 2 g.

TORTA RUSTICA

Serves 6

This torta is a hearty breakfast and also a terrific brunch or lunch dish served with some fresh spinach salad on the side. Based on a traditional Italian holiday torta, this mix is usually baked encased in pastry dough. My version is lighter and easier to make and perhaps even tastier than its Italian cousin.

3 tablespoons extra virgin olive oil

1 small onion, grated

1 teaspoon finely chopped garlic

650 g (1 lb 7 oz) spinach, cooked, chopped, and well drained (see Note)

240 g (8½ oz) sheep's milk ricotta cheese

60 g (2 oz) pecorino romano cheese, grated

Salt and pepper

Preheat the oven to maximum.

Generously butter a 2-liter (3½-pint) casserole. Set aside.

Place the olive oil in a small frying pan over medium heat. Add the onion and garlic and sauté for about 3 minutes or just until softened. Remove from the heat and set aside.

Combine the spinach with the ricotta and pecorino in a mixing bowl. Add the reserved onion mixture, season with salt and pepper to taste, and stir to blend completely. Scrape the mixture into the prepared casserole, smoothing the top with a spatula.

Transfer to the preheated oven and bake for 5 minutes; then, lower the heat to 180ºC/350ºF/Gas Mark 4 and bake for an additional 20 minutes or until completely set and golden brown around the edges.

NOTE You can use 340 g (12 oz) frozen chopped organic spinach if you thaw it completely and carefully squeeze out all of the liquid. If the spinach is too wet, the torta won't set properly.

Nutritional Analysis per Serving: calories 222, carbohydrates 11 g, fiber 2 g, protein 14 g, fat 20 g, sodium 338 mg, sugar 2 g.

LUNCH

If you normally eat lunch in a restaurant or company cafeteria, now is the time to start "brown bagging" it. Although you can often find unadulterated dishes to order when you eat out, it's far better to lunch on something you've made at home using the best possible ingredients. Soups and stews can often be eaten at room temperature or packed in a thermos; salads can be put together and dressed when you are ready to eat; and many of the more complicated dishes can be made for a lunch or brunch or even dinner at home and then the leftovers used to create a healthy lunch for the next day. I almost guarantee that if you share your brown bag with your co-workers you will soon have everyone following your diet.

Really Great Tomato Soup
Mushroom-Hazelnut Soup
Winter Squash Soup
Chilled Avocado Soup
Coconut-Chicken Soup
Texas-Style Chilli
Curried Pork Stew
Green Mango, Watercress, and Rocket Salad
Avocado-Walnut Salad
Caesar Salad with Asiago Tuiles
Tomatoes with Mozzarella, Avocado, and Basil
Greek Salad

Chef's Salad Bowl

Tuscan Salad

Beef and Watercress Salad

Thai Pork Lettuce Cups

Warm Swiss Chard, Pancetta, and Almond Salad

Tomatoes Stuffed with Prawn Salad

Prawn and Celery Salad

Niçoise Salad

Salmon-Avocado Salad

Kale and Bacon Frittata

Shakshuka or Eggs in Purgatory

Wild Mushroom Gratin

Cheese Soufflé

Falafel with Tahini Sauce

Spicy Chicken Burgers with Guacamole

Almond-Crusted Chicken Strips

The Best Beef 'n' Cheese Burgers

Garlic-Herb Mussels

REALLY GREAT TOMATO SOUP

Serves 6

Perfectly ripe and juicy tomatoes give this soup the intense flavor you need; big, fat, deep red beefsteaks are the best. If there are fresh herbs that you particularly like, add them to the onions or use them as a garnish. Basil, of course, is the perfect mate for ripe tomatoes. A slice or two of fresh green chilli will add a bit of heat if that's to your liking.

115 g (4 oz) unsalted butter

225 g (8 oz) onions, peeled and chopped

1 teaspoon finely chopped garlic

2.7 kg (6 lb) very ripe tomatoes, cored and chopped

Salt and pepper

Crumbled feta cheese for garnish, optional

Heat the butter in a large saucepan over medium heat. Add the onions and garlic, lower the heat, and cook, stirring frequently, for about 20 minutes or until soft and fragrant, but not colored.

Add the tomatoes and season with salt and pepper to taste. Raise the heat to medium-low and continue to cook, stirring frequently, for about 25 minutes or until the tomatoes are mushy and the mixture soupy.

Remove from the heat and transfer to a blender. Process until smooth. This may have to be done in batches. Be sure to hold the top of the blender down with a kitchen towel as the pressure from the hot liquid can push the lid up.

When all of the soup has been puréed, pour it through a fine mesh sieve into a clean nonreactive saucepan. Taste and, if necessary, season with additional salt and pepper. Return to medium heat and cook until hot.

Remove from the heat and ladle into shallow soup bowls. Sprinkle with feta cheese, if desired, and serve.

Nutritional Analysis per Serving (about 375 ml/13 fl oz): calories 224, carbohydrates 20 g, fiber 6 g, protein 4 g, fat 16 g, sodium 409 mg, sugar 13 g.

MUSHROOM-HAZELNUT SOUP

Serves 6

When I first tasted this soup I experienced an intriguing mix of flavors on my palate. It is a trickster – you get a hint of hazelnut, but when the nuts blend into the mushroom a unique, umami flavor is revealed. You can make it with either chicken stock for a rich soup or with vegetable stock for a lighter lunch. If you only need one serving, it keeps well, covered and refrigerated, and will taste even better when warmed up a day or two later. If you want to move it to the dinner table, top it with slices of grilled pork sausage and a mound of fried thinly sliced shiitake mushrooms along with a garnish of chopped flat-leaf parsley or tarragon.

55 g (2 oz) unsalted butter
450 g (1 lb) onions, peeled and sliced
565 g (1 lb 4 oz) chestnut mushrooms, cleaned and cut into pieces
750 ml-1 liter (1¼-1¾ pints) chicken stock (low-sodium if desired)
    plus more if needed
85 g (3 oz) toasted hazelnuts, finely ground
Salt and pepper

Heat the butter in a large saucepan over medium-low heat. Add the onions and cook, stirring frequently, for about 12 minutes or until soft and translucent. Add the mushrooms and continue to cook, stirring frequently, for 10 minutes. Add enough chicken stock to barely cover, raise the heat, and bring to a simmer. Immediately reduce the heat and simmer for an additional 10 minutes.

Remove from the heat and stir in the nuts. Pour into a blender and process until smooth. You may have to add more chicken stock to reach a smooth soup consistency. This may have to be done in batches. Be sure to hold the top of the blender down with a kitchen towel as the pressure from the hot liquid can push the lid up.

Pour the soup into a clean saucepan and place over medium heat until very hot. Remove from the heat, season and serve.

Nutritional Analysis per Serving (about 250 ml/8 fl oz): calories 198, carbohydrates 14 g, fiber 3 g, protein 6 g, fat 15 g, sodium 41 mg, sugar 5 g.

WINTER SQUASH SOUP

Serves 6

Perfect for a fall or winter day when there is a chill in the air, with the heat from the ginger and chilli balancing the sweetness of the squash. It is also a beautiful soup for a dinner party, pale orange highlighted with a few dots of cream and chives as garnish. The soup may be made ahead of time and stored, covered and refrigerated, for up to 3 days, or frozen for up to 2 months.

Since this soup is relatively high in carbohydrates, take care about the remainder of your total carbohydrate intake for the day.

2 medium squash, such as butternut, kabocha, or hubbard, peeled, halved, seeded, and cubed

115 g (4 oz) shallots, peeled and chopped

1 teaspoon grated ginger root

1 teaspoon finely chopped fresh green chilli

$1/2$ teaspoon curry powder

$1/4$ teaspoon ground nutmeg

$1/4$ teaspoon ground cinnamon

$1/4$ teaspoon ground cardamom

Salt and white pepper

1.2 liters (2 pints) chicken stock (low-sodium if desired)

2 tablespoons double cream, optional

1 tablespoon finely chopped chives or flat-leaf parsley, optional

Combine the squash cubes, shallots, and ginger in a steamer basket placed over boiling water. Cover and steam for about 15 minutes or until the squash is very tender.

Transfer the squash mixture to a food processor fitted with the metal blade. This may have to be done in batches. Process to a smooth purée. As the squash is puréed, transfer it to a large saucepan.

When all of the squash is puréed, add the chilli, curry powder, nutmeg, cinnamon, and cardamom to the pan along with salt and white pepper to taste. Add the chicken stock and place over medium-high heat. Bring to a simmer; then, lower the heat and simmer for about 20 minutes or until the flavors have blended.

Serve hot, garnished with just a few dots of double cream and a sprinkle of chopped chives or flat-leaf parsley, if desired.

Nutritional Analysis per Serving (500 ml/17 fl oz): calories 162, carbohydrates 39 g, fiber 7 g, protein 5 g, fat 0 g, sodium 170 mg, sugar 9 g.

CHILLED AVOCADO SOUP

Serves 2

This soup is delicious unadorned, but if you feel like getting fancy, a little mound of crab or lobster meat, a beautiful large prawn, or even a few pieces of avocado in the center make it dinner-party ready. It is light and refreshing and the beneficial avocado makes it a star in the *Grain Brain* diet.

I've made the recipe for only 2 servings so that it remains a glorious pale green. If you are serving more than two people it can easily be doubled or tripled, but it can't sit around for very long as the color darkens and isn't nearly as pleasing.

1 large ripe avocado, peeled, pitted, and diced

100 g (3½ oz) cucumber, peeled, seeds removed, and diced

350 ml (12 fl oz) cold chicken stock (low-sodium if desired)

2 tablespoons lime juice

4 tablespoons cold unsweetened almond milk

Salt

Tabasco sauce

Chopped mint leaves for garnish, optional

Place the avocado and cucumber in a blender jar. Add the chicken stock and lime juice and process until smooth.

Pour into a clean bowl and stir in the almond milk, salt, and Tabasco.

Serve immediately, garnished with chopped mint, if desired, or cover and refrigerate for no more than 3 hours or the soup will begin to discolor.

Nutritional Analysis per Serving (about 600 ml/1 pint): calories 166, carbohydrates 10 g, fiber 6 g, protein 4 g, fat 14 g, sodium 380 mg, sugar 1 g.

COCONUT-CHICKEN SOUP

Serves 6

Another elementary soup that makes a delicious and quick lunch. For the protein, you can substitute prawns or salmon if you like. Don't panic if you can't find the kaffir lime leaves or lemongrass; I've given you substitutions that still make it doable. However, most Asian markets carry lime leaves and lemongrass frozen and they are certainly available online.

850 ml (1½ pints) chicken stock (low-sodium if desired)

2 tablespoons fish sauce (nam pla)

2 tablespoons lemon juice

1 tablespoon lime juice

6 kaffir lime leaves or the zest of 1 lime combined with 2 bay
    leaves

200 g (7 oz) tomatoes, peeled, seeded, and diced

1 tablespoon finely chopped lemongrass or 1 strip lemon peel
    combined with a few flat-leaf parsley stems

3 x 3-mm ($\frac{1}{8}$-inch) thick slices ginger root

1 tablespoon finely chopped red or green chillies or to taste

375 ml (13 fl oz) unsweetened coconut milk

1 large boneless, skinless chicken breast, cut into thin strips

1 bunch enoki mushrooms, tough stems removed

3 tablespoons chopped coriander

1 tablespoon chopped mint leaves

Combine the chicken stock with the fish sauce and lemon and lime juices in a large saucepan. Add the kaffir lime leaves, tomato, lemon-grass, ginger, and chillies over medium heat. Bring to a simmer and add the coconut milk along with the chicken strips and mushrooms. Return to the simmer and cook for about 7 minutes or until the chicken is just cooked through. Do not allow the soup to come to a boil or overcook or the chicken will be tough and the broth will separate slightly.

Remove from the heat and stir in the coriander and mint. Serve immediately.

Nutritional Analysis per Serving (300 ml/$\frac{1}{2}$ pint): calories 210, carbohydrates 5 g, fiber 1 g, protein 20 g, fat 12 g, sodium 563mg, sugar 1 g.

TEXAS-STYLE CHILLI

Serves 6

In Texas, unlike other parts of America, real chilli does not contain beans. This is about as pure a Texas chilli as you can get – one that could have been found out on the range during a cattle run. You can serve with some freshly chopped red onions, coriander, and hot chillies as toppings to take the flavor up a notch or two if you wish. For an even richer flavor, an ounce of dark (over 70% cacao) chocolate added with the meat will add intensity and depth.

7 dried chillies, such as a mix of ancho, pasilla, or guajillo, stemmed and seeded

85 g (3 oz) beef dripping, suet, or ghee

900 g (2 lb) stewing steak, coarsely chopped

Salt and pepper

450 g (1 lb) onions, diced

2 tablespoons finely chopped garlic

1 tablespoon finely chopped jalapeño chilli or to taste

1 tablespoon ground cumin

1 teaspoon dried oregano

1.2 liters (2 pints) beef stock (low-sodium if desired)

2 tablespoons chopped coriander

1 tablespoon lime juice

50 g (1¾ oz) queso fresco or other dry crumbly white cheese, grated

Combine the dried chillies with 500 ml (17 fl oz) water in a medium saucepan over high heat. Bring to a boil; then, lower the heat and simmer, stirring occasionally, for about 10 minutes or until the chillies are very soft. Remove from the heat and set aside to cool slightly.

Pour the chillies along with their cooking liquid into a blender. You may not need all of the liquid as you need just enough liquid to make a thick purée.

Heat the dripping in a large saucepan over medium-high heat. Add the stewing steak, season with salt and pepper to taste and fry, stirring frequently, for 5 minutes or just until brown.

Using a slotted spoon, transfer the meat to a bowl. Do not take the pan off the heat.

To the hot pan, add the onion, garlic, chilli, cumin, and oregano and cook, stirring frequently, for about 6 minutes or until just beginning to brown. Add the reserved dried chilli purée and cook, stirring frequently, for about 4 minutes or until very dark and quite thick. Take care that the mixture does not scorch on the bottom of the pan.

Stir in the reserved meat along with the stock. Bring to a boil and then lower the heat and simmer for 1 hour or until reduced by half and very thick.

Remove from the heat and stir in the coriander and lime juice. Taste and, if necessary, season with additional salt and pepper.

Serve sprinkled with cheese.

Nutritional Analysis per Serving: calories 606, carbohydrates 18 g, fiber 6 g, protein 45 g, fat 40 g, sodium 598 mg, sugar 4 g.

CURRIED PORK STEW

Serves 4

This is a quick and uncomplicated lunch stew. It keeps, covered and refrigerated, for a few days, so if you only need lunch for one, make it anyway . . . it will be a fast reheat for lunch on another day or a very tasty side dish for grilled fish or poultry at dinner time.

2 tablespoons coconut oil

340 g (12 oz) lean pork, cut into small cubes

450 g (1 lb) onions, peeled and chopped

1 tablespoon finely chopped garlic

1 teaspoon finely chopped jalapeño or other hot green chilli or to
    taste

1 tablespoon hot curry powder

$\frac{1}{2}$ teaspoon cayenne pepper

Pinch ground turmeric

310 g (11 oz) organic spinach

850 ml (1½ pints) unsweetened coconut milk

Salt

Heat the oil in a large saucepan over medium heat. When hot but not smoking, add the pork, onion, garlic, and chilli, stirring to blend. Fry, stirring frequently, for 6 minutes or until the pork has cooked through and the aromatics have softened; then sprinkle in the curry powder, cayenne, and turmeric and stir to incorporate.

Add the spinach and, using tongs, toss to coat the spinach with the onion mixture. Stir in the coconut milk, season with salt, and bring to a simmer.

Remove from the heat and serve.

Nutritional Analysis per Serving: calories 612, carbohydrates 22 g, fiber 4 g, protein 23 g, fat 49 g, sodium 454 mg, sugar 4 g.

GREEN MANGO, WATERCRESS, AND ROCKET SALAD

Serves 6

I find this salad refreshing since the green mangoes are not at all sugary. The tongue-tingling chillies and the peppery greens contrast beautifully with the sweet-tartness of the mango. The popularity of Thai cooking has brought green mangoes to the neighborhood supermarket, but if you can't find them, replace them with under-ripe pears.

2 teaspoons stevia

Juice of 3 limes

1 teaspoon sesame oil

4 red birds' eye chillies or other small, hot red chillies, stemmed, seeded, and finely chopped

Salt

285 g (10 oz) watercress, tough ends removed

85 g (3 oz) baby rocket leaves

2 large green mangoes

1 tablespoon black sesame seeds, optional

Place the stevia in a small nonstick saucepan over low heat. Cook, stirring frequently, for just a minute or so or just until it has melted completely. Remove from the heat and whisk in the lime juice and sesame oil. Add the chillies and stir to combine. Season with salt to taste. Set aside to cool.

Combine the watercress and rocket in a large mixing bowl. Set aside.

Peel the mangoes and then cut the flesh into julienne strips. Toss the mango strips with the watercress and rocket. Pour the cooled sauce over the top and toss to combine.

Mound equal portions of the salad in the center of each of 6 salad plates. Sprinkle with sesame seeds, if desired, and serve.

Nutritional Analysis per Serving: calories 55, carbohydrates 11g, fiber 1 g, protein 2 g, fat 1 g, sodium 614 mg, sugar 8 g.

AVOCADO-WALNUT SALAD

Serves 2

Throughout the Middle East you will find salads made with a combination of nuts and fruits or vegetables. This is one of my favorites. Just be sure to toast the walnuts as that will give them the extra crunch they need to offset the creamy avocado.

Since this salad is relatively high in carbohydrates, take care about the remainder of your total carbohydrate intake for the day.

75-100 g (about 3 oz) celeriac (or celery), diced

125 g (4½ oz) cucumber, diced (see Note)

75 g (2³/₄ oz) toasted walnuts, chopped, plus more for garnish, if desired

55 g (2 oz) sweet onion, peeled and finely diced

1 avocado, peeled, pitted, and cut into chunks

125 ml (4 fl oz) Spiced Vinaigrette (see page 36) or vinaigrette of your choice

1 head romaine lettuce, cut, lengthwise, into long, thin strips

Combine the celeriac, cucumber, walnuts, and onion in a medium mixing bowl, tossing to blend. Add the avocado and, using about half of the vinaigrette, lightly dress the mix.

Place the romaine on a serving plate and dress with the remaining vinaigrette. Mound the avocado salad on top and serve garnished with additional toasted walnuts, if desired.

NOTE Sometimes organic cucumbers can be difficult to find. In this case, replace the cucumber with an equal portion of celery, radishes, or water chestnuts.

Nutritional Analysis per Serving: calories 832, carbohydrates 36 g, fiber 77 g, protein 16 g, fat 77 g, sodium 313 mg, sugar 11 g.

CAESAR SALAD WITH ASIAGO TUILES

Serves 2

If you go the extra distance and make the Asiago Tuiles (just a fancy French name for a thin wafer), you will never miss the croutons that usually garnish a Caesar Salad. If you are looking for a more substantial lunch, top each serving with a poached egg garnished with 2 anchovy fillets.

Salt

1 clove garlic, peeled

1 medium head romaine lettuce, chopped

1 large egg yolk, beaten

4 tablespoons lemon juice

1 tablespoon white wine vinegar

1 teaspoon mustard powder

250 ml (8 fl oz) extra virgin olive oil

3 anchovy fillets, well-drained and chopped

4 tablespoons grated Parmesan cheese

1 tablespoon finely chopped capers

White pepper

Asiago Tuiles (recipe follows)

Sprinkle about a tablespoon of salt into a wooden salad bowl. Using the garlic clove, rub the salt into the bowl so that it is seasoned with garlic. Then, wipe the salt out of the bowl and add the lettuce.

Combine the egg yolk with the lemon juice, vinegar, and mustard powder in a blender and process to blend. With the motor running, slowly add the oil, processing until well emulsified.

Pour into a small bowl and whisk in the anchovies, cheese, and capers. Taste and adjust the seasoning with salt and pepper.

Pour just enough of the dressing over the lettuce to lightly coat and toss to combine. Serve with 4 Asiago Tuiles (2 per person) on the side.

ASIAGO TUILES

50 g (1³/₄ oz) Asiago (or Parmesan) cheese, grated

Preheat the oven to 160ºC/325ºF/Gas mark 3.

Line a baking tray with parchment paper.

Place a 5-cm (2-inch) round cookie cutter on the parchment paper and sprinkle an even layer of cheese (about 1 tablespoon) inside the circle. Continue making cheese circles, leaving about 5 cm (2 inches) between each one, until you have made 8. You will only need 4 but, you may have some breakage, plus they are a delicious snack.

Place the tray in the preheated oven. Bake for about 4 minutes or until the cheese circles have melted into 5-cm (2-inch) solid disks.

Remove from the oven and set aside to cool.

Using a spatula, carefully remove the disks from the baking tray, keeping them whole. Do take care because the disks are quite fragile. If not using immediately, store, separated by greaseproof paper, absolutely airtight, for up to 1 day.

Nutritional Analysis per Serving (includes dressing and 2 tuiles): calories 346, carbohydrates 12 g, fiber 7 g, protein 12 g, fat 30 g, sodium 489 mg, sugar 4 g.

TOMATOES WITH MOZZARELLA, AVOCADO, AND BASIL

Serves 2

This is a bit more substantial than the usual "caprese" salad as it has avocado in the mix. The buffalo mozzarella adds a milky richness that melds right into the creamy avocado.

2 ripe tomatoes, cored and thinly sliced, crosswise

225 g (8 oz) fresh buffalo mozzarella

1 large avocado, peeled, pitted, and thinly sliced

4 tablespoons extra virgin olive oil

2 tablespoons red wine vinegar

Salt and pepper

2 tablespoons chopped basil leaves

Lay alternate slices of tomato, mozzarella, and avocado around the outside edge of each of 2 luncheon plates. You should have enough remaining to make another concentric circle in the center of the plate.

Drizzle with olive oil and a few splashes of vinegar. Season with salt and pepper to taste and sprinkle the basil over all.

Serve immediately.

Nutritional Analysis per Serving: calories 775, carbohydrates 20 g, fiber 9 g, protein 28 g, fat 77 g, sodium 121 mg, sugar 6 g.

GREEK SALAD

Serves 4

The better the tomatoes, the better this salad. You want them ripe, juicy, and straight-off-the-vine for maximum flavor. Of course, it would be best if you could walk out of the door and pick them in your garden – don't we all wish this were so? I like meaty Greek olives in the salad, although in Greece this would be a no-no.

2 ripe tomatoes, cored and cut into chunks

1 medium cucumber, peeled and cut into chunks

1 small red onion, peeled and cut, lengthwise, into slivers

120 g (4¼ oz) sheep's milk feta cheese, diced

85 g (3 oz) pitted Greek olives

2 teaspoons well-drained capers

4 tablespoons Italian Vinaigrette (see page 36)

255 g (9 oz) romaine lettuce, chopped

1 teaspoon dried oregano

Combine the tomatoes, cucumber, and onion in a mixing bowl. Add the cheese, olives, and capers, tossing gently to blend. Drizzle with the vinaigrette and again toss to coat.

Place an equal portion of the lettuce on each of 4 luncheon plates. Mound the tomato salad on top. Sprinkle with oregano and serve.

Nutritional Analysis per Serving: calories 319, carbohydrates 21 g, fiber 10 g, protein 13 g, fat 24 g, sodium 794 mg, sugar 8 g.

CHEF'S SALAD BOWL

Serves 4

This is a complete meal in a bowl and quick to put together since no cooking is required – except for the hard-boiled eggs, which you should keep on hand for a little snack or pick-me-up. You should always serve a chef's salad with the ingredients beautifully arranged on top and toss it at the last minute.

255 g (9 oz) crisp lettuce, such as organic romaine or iceberg,
    roughly chopped
75 ml (3 fl oz) Basic Vinaigrette (see page 34)
115 g (4 oz) rare roast beef, cut into strips
225 g (8 oz) turkey breast, cut into strips
115 g (4 oz) Emmental cheese, cut into strips
115 g (4 oz) Cheddar cheese, cut into strips
2 large hard-boiled eggs, peeled and quartered (see Note)
4 ripe plum tomatoes, peeled, cored, and thinly sliced crosswise
1 avocado, peeled, pitted, and thinly sliced
2 radishes, trimmed and thinly sliced

Place the lettuce in a large wooden salad bowl. Drizzle about half of the vinaigrette over the top and toss to lightly coat.

Place the roast beef in a circle around the edge of the salad bowl. Then, moving inward, make a circle of turkey. Place the Emmental and Cheddar in equal mounds in the center of the ring of meats.

Place the egg quarters equidistant around the edge of the roast beef. Then, place a circle of tomato and avocado between the roast beef and turkey followed by a circle of radish between the turkey and the cheeses.

After presenting at the table, toss, and serve immediately with the extra dressing on the side.

NOTE To make perfect hard-boiled eggs, place the eggs in a saucepan with cold water to cover by at least 2.5 cm (1 inch). Place over high heat and bring to just a boil. Immediately remove from the heat and cover. Let stand for 15 minutes; then, drain off the hot water and place the pan under cold running water. Continue running cold water until the eggs are cold. Crack the shells in random spots and peel, from the largest end down, under cold running water.

Nutritional Analysis per Serving: calories 667, carbohydrates 19 g, fiber 11 g, protein 49 g, fat 46 g, sodium 396 mg, sugar 6 g.

TUSCAN SALAD

Serves 4

The Tuscan hills are the backdrop for this very tasty salad, mainly because that is where you will find one of the oldest and largest breeds of cattle still being bred – the Chianina. Their meat is highly prized for its richness and nutritional value and, of course, the most highly prized animals are grass-fed, just as they were centuries ago. When not in Tuscany any grass-fed beef will be an excellent substitute.

450 g (1 lb) cooked roast beef, cubed

1 red onion, peeled and cut into thin strips

1 large ripe tomato, cored, seeded, and chopped

4 tablespoons chopped anchovies (either olive-oil packed or salt-packed, your choice)

4 tablespoons Balsamic Vinaigrette (see page 35)

325 g (11½ oz) mixed bitter salad leaves, such as endive, rocket, escarole, or radicchio, washed and dried

4 tablespoons torn basil leaves

2 tablespoons capers, optional

Place the beef in a mixing bowl. Add the onion, tomato, and

anchovies, stirring to combine. Add the vinaigrette, tossing to lightly coat.

Combine the salad leaves with the basil on a serving platter, tossing to blend. Scoop the beef mixture over the leaves. If desired, sprinkle with capers and serve.

VARIATIONS The salad can be made with roast pork or roast chicken or turkey.

Nutritional Analysis per Serving: calories 386, carbohydrates 8 g, fiber 3 g, protein 35 g, fat 25 g, sodium 447 mg, sugar 2 g.

BEEF AND WATERCRESS SALAD

Serves 4

Just a tad spicy, but a first-rate combo – fatty beef, herbaceous watercress, zesty citrus, topped off with fragrant fresh herbs and crunchy bits of coconut. Who could ask for more?

450 g (1 lb) cooked rare roast beef, cut into 1-cm (½-inch) thick strips

2 bunches watercress, well washed and dried, tough stems removed

1 medium red onion, peeled and thinly sliced

135 g (4¾ oz) radishes, sliced

5 tablespoons melted coconut oil

2 tablespoons lime juice

1 teaspoon chilli powder

1 teaspoon finely chopped garlic

¼ teaspoon cayenne pepper

4 tablespoons toasted coconut flakes

4 tablespoons coriander leaves

4 tablespoons mint leaves

Combine the beef with the watercress, onion, and radishes in a large mixing bowl.

Whisk the oil and juice together. When blended, whisk in the chilli powder, garlic, and cayenne. Pour the dressing over the beef mixture, tossing to evenly coat.

Scoop the salad onto a serving plate and sprinkle the coconut, coriander, and mint over the top. Serve immediately.

Nutritional Analysis per Serving: calories 468, carbohydrates 5 g, fiber 1 g, protein 31 g, fat 34 g, sodium 54 mg, sugar 2 g.

THAI PORK LETTUCE CUPS

Serves 4

This zesty mix makes a light and refreshing lunch that is painless to put together. It can be served on the lettuce leaves, as I suggest here, but it can also be wrapped in lettuce leaves for gluten-free spring rolls. Minced chicken, turkey, or lamb may be substituted for the pork.

1 tablespoon coconut oil

450 g (1 lb) lean minced pork

2 tablespoons finely chopped shallot

1 tablespoon finely chopped garlic

2 tablespoons finely chopped red onion

2 tablespoons finely chopped mint leaves

1 tablespoon finely chopped spring onion

1 tablespoon finely chopped coriander

1 tablespoon finely chopped hot red chilli or to taste

1 tablespoon lime juice

1 tablespoon fish sauce (nam pla)

Salt

12 large round lettuce leaves

4 mint sprigs for garnish

Heat the oil in a large frying pan over medium heat. Add the pork, shallots, and garlic and fry, stirring frequently, for about 8 minutes or until the pork is crumbly and cooked through.

Remove from the heat and scrape into a mixing bowl. Add the onion, chopped mint, spring onion, coriander, and chilli, stirring to blend. Add the lime juice and fish sauce and blend well. Taste and, if necessary, season with salt.

Place 3 lettuce leaves in the center of each of 4 luncheon plates. Mound an equal portion of the pork mixture into the center. Garnish with a mint sprig and serve.

Nutritional Analysis per Serving: calories 267, carbohydrates 5 g, fiber 1 g, protein 37 g, fat 11 g, sodium 529 mg, sugar 2 g.

WARM SWISS CHARD, PANCETTA, AND ALMOND SALAD

Serves 4

The warm pancetta and dressing slightly wilt the chard, keeping it fresh-tasting but not quite raw. If you use rainbow chard, the salad is visually so appealing, and the marriage of the soft chard, toasty almonds, and crisp pancetta makes it taste as good as it looks.

1 bunch rainbow Swiss chard, tough stems removed and torn into
    pieces

225 g (8 oz) pancetta, diced

2 tablespoons extra virgin olive oil

3 tablespoons red wine vinegar

1 tablespoon grainy mustard

Cracked black pepper

140 g (5 oz) unblanched almonds, toasted and chopped

Place the chard into a large heatproof salad bowl. Set aside.

Place the pancetta and oil in a large frying pan over medium-low heat. Fry, stirring frequently, for about 12 minutes or until all of the fat has rendered out and the pancetta is brown and crisp. Using a slotted spoon, transfer the pancetta to a double layer of kitchen paper to drain.

Using a whisk, beat the vinegar and mustard into the pancetta fat in the pan. Season with cracked black pepper. Pour the dressing over the chard and add the almonds and warm pancetta, tossing to combine.

Serve while still warm.

NOTE For those on a restricted sodium diet, the pancetta can be eliminated from the recipe.

Nutritional Analysis per Serving: calories 513, carbohydrates 15 g, fiber 6 g, protein 18 g, fat 43 g, sodium 1250 mg, sugar 3 g.

TOMATOES STUFFED WITH PRAWN SALAD

Serves 4

When friends gather, this is an exceptional lunch as it takes no time to prepare, but looks as though the cook has spent hours making it. In place of the prawns, cooked lobster, line-caught tuna, or free-range, organic chicken or turkey will make an equally tasty filling. If you want to fancy it up a bit, make a little avocado salsa to top it off. All that is required is 1 diced avocado with a toss of finely chopped onion, chopped coriander, and lime juice.

4 large ripe tomatoes

1 ripe avocado, peeled, pitted, and chopped

1 teaspoon lime juice

Tabasco sauce

225 g (8 oz) peeled and deveined cooked prawns, roughly chopped

4 tablespoons Mayonnaise (see page 38)

1 tablespoon finely chopped spring onion with some green part

Salt and pepper

8 round lettuce leaves

4 coriander sprigs for garnish

Cut the top quarter off each tomato. Scoop out the seeds and pulp and place the tomatoes, cut side down, on a double layer of kitchen paper to drain for at least 15 minutes.

Place the avocado in a shallow bowl, add the lime juice and Tabasco, and, using a kitchen fork, mash until quite smooth.

Place the prawns in a medium mixing bowl. Add the mashed avocado along with the mayonnaise and spring onion. Season with salt and pepper to taste and gently toss to completely blend. Stuff an equal portion of the salad into each tomato, mounding it slightly.

Place the lettuce leaves in the center of each of 4 plates. Place a tomato in the center of the leaves on each plate, garnish with a sprig of coriander, and serve.

Nutritional Analysis per Serving: calories 267, carbohydrates 13 g, fiber 6 g, protein 13 g, fat 20 g, sodium 542 mg, sugar 6 g.

PRAWN AND CELERY SALAD

Serves 4

This citrusy, slightly tongue-tingling dressing is a rich cover for the sweet prawns and crisp vegetables. You can make this salad with cooked wild-caught meaty fish, such as halibut, free-range chicken or turkey breast, or pasture-raised, organic pork.

125 ml (4 fl oz) Mayonnaise (see page 38)

1 tablespoon lime juice

1 tablespoon lemon juice

2 teaspoons hot curry powder

450 g (1 lb) cooked medium prawns, peeled and deveined

2 ribs celery, well washed, peeled, and cut in thin slices on the bias

150 g (5¼ oz) fennel, diced

2 tablespoons chopped spring onions

Pepper

240 g (8½ oz) mixed salad leaves, well washed, dried, and chopped

1 tablespoon snipped chives, optional

Combine the mayonnaise with the citrus juices and curry powder in a medium mixing bowl, whisking to blend well.

Add the prawns along with the celery, fennel, and spring onions. Toss to lightly coat and season with pepper.

Place the salad leaves down the center of a small serving platter. Mound the salad on top. Sprinkle with chives if desired and serve.

NOTE For those on a restricted sodium diet, the prawns can be replaced with chunks of fresh, barely cooked tuna.

Nutritional Analysis per Serving: calories 332, carbohydrates 11 g, fiber 4 g, protein 23 g, fat 24 g, sodium 884 mg, sugar 1 g.

NIÇOISE SALAD

Serves 4

Classically, a French *Salade Niçoise* should have slices of new potatoes as a component. I've used artichoke hearts as a replacement and find that the flavor seems even more typically Provençal than potatoes.

450-g (1-lb) piece yellowfin tuna

Salt and pepper

2 tablespoons coconut oil

4 cooked fresh, jarred, or canned artichoke hearts, quartered

2 medium beefsteak tomatoes, cored, seeded, and roughly chopped

85 g (3 oz) niçoise olives, pitted

240 g (8½ oz) gourmet salad leaves or other mixed baby salad
   leaves

75 ml (3 fl oz) Balsamic Vinaigrette (see page 35)

115 g (4 oz) cooked haricots verts or small green or yellow beans

4 hard-boiled large eggs (see page 80), peeled and quartered

1 piece Parmesan cheese for shaving

Lightly score one side of the tuna and season with salt and pepper
to taste.

Heat the oil in a medium heavy frying pan over high heat. When the
oil is smoking, add the tuna, scored side down. Sear for 3 minutes; then
turn and sear on the other side for 2 minutes or just until nicely colored
but still almost raw in the center. Remove from the heat and place on a
double layer of kitchen paper to drain. Allow to cool slightly.

Combine the artichoke hearts, tomatoes, and olives in a mixing
bowl, stirring to blend well.

Place the salad leaves in a large bowl. Add just enough vinaigrette
to lightly coat, tossing to blend. Transfer the dressed leaves to a
serving platter and mound the artichoke/tomato mixture in the
center.

Using a sharp knife, cut the tuna, crosswise, into 5-mm (¼-inch) thick
slices. Place the slices, slightly overlapping, around the edge of the salad
leaves. Place the haricots verts and hard-boiled eggs around the salad in
an attractive pattern. Shave a few pieces of Parmesan cheese over the
top, drizzle the remaining vinaigrette over all, and serve.

Nutritional Analysis per Serving: calories 442, carbohydrates 14 g, fiber 5 g,
protein 36 g, fat 32 g, sodium 347 mg, sugar 4 g.

SALMON-AVOCADO SALAD

Serves 2

Light and extremely healthy, this salad could also be made with left-over salmon. The sesame seeds look great and add a hint of nuttiness, but they really wouldn't be missed if you happened to have some grilled salmon waiting to be used. The sprouts add a nice bite; just make sure you get vegetable sprouts, not ones from legumes or wheat.

If you have black sesame seeds on hand, they look splendid sprinkled on the salad just before serving.

1 x 225 g (8 oz) skinless salmon fillet

Salt and pepper

2 teaspoons sesame seeds

3 tablespoons toasted sesame oil

1 tablespoon champagne vinegar

85 g (3 oz) baby rocket

35 g (1¼ oz) green seed sprouts (preferably radish, but all types except mung bean, lentil, or wheat can be used)

70 g (2½ oz) red radishes, thinly sliced

1 avocado, peeled, pitted, and thinly sliced

Preheat a nonstick ridged griddle pan over medium-high heat.

Season the salmon with salt and pepper to taste and then sprinkle with sesame seeds, pressing down to adhere to the flesh. Place the salmon into the hot pan and grill, turning once, for about 10 minutes or until just barely cooked through. Remove from the heat and set aside to cool slightly.

Combine the sesame oil and vinegar in a small bowl. Season with salt and pepper to taste and whisk to blend.

Combine the rocket, seed sprouts, and radish in a mixing bowl. Drizzle with just enough of the sesame dressing to coat very lightly. Toss to mix well.

Manchego Tortilla (page 58)

Eggs Benedict with Courgette Pancakes (page 52)

Thai Pork Lettuce Cups (page 82)

Tomatoes with Mozzarella, Avocado, and Basil (page 77)

Shakshuka, Eggs in Purgatory (page 90)

Salmon-Avocado Salad (page 88)

Green Beans with Walnuts (page 135)

Sautéed Cherry Tomatoes in Herbs (page 125)

Roasted Mixed Vegetables (page 106)

Place an equal portion of the dressed salad on each of 2 serving plates. Pull the salmon apart into chunks and place it over the salad. Garnish with avocado slices and drizzle the remaining dressing over the salmon and avocado.

Serve immediately.

Nutritional Analysis per Serving: calories 512, carbohydrates 13 g, fiber 8 g, protein 27 g, fat 42 g, sodium 686 mg, sugar 1 g.

KALE AND BACON FRITTATA

Serves 4

The egg mixture can be used with almost any combination of vegetable and/or meat. Some good suggestions are broccoli/mushroom, pumpkin/mint, tomato/basil, courgette/feta, ham/Gruyère cheese, Cheddar cheese/bacon – well, you see how it goes; the list is long and the flavors inviting.

5 large eggs

115 g (4 oz) kale (or Swiss chard or spinach), finely chopped

225 g (8 oz) cooked bacon, chopped

4 tablespoons grated Parmesan cheese

Salt and pepper

2 large egg whites

Preheat the oven to 180ºC/350ºF/Gas Mark 4.

Generously butter a 20-cm (8-inch) ovenproof frying pan. Set aside.

Place the eggs in a medium mixing bowl, whisking to blend. Add the kale and bacon and season with 2 tablespoons of the cheese, salt, and pepper.

Using a hand-held electric mixer, beat the egg whites until just firm, but not dry. Fold the beaten egg whites into the egg mixture just until small pieces of egg white remain.

Scrape the mixture into the prepared pan. Sprinkle the top with the remaining cheese and transfer to the preheated oven.

Bake for about 18 minutes or until the center is set and the top is golden brown and almost crisp around the edges.

Remove from the oven and let stand for a couple of minutes before cutting into wedges and serving.

Nutritional Analysis per Serving: calories 238, carbohydrates 4 g, fiber 1 g, protein 18 g, fat 16 g, sodium 653 mg, sugar 1 g.

SHAKSHUKA OR EGGS IN PURGATORY

Serves 4

Throughout the Middle East and Northern Africa you will find some version of this dish, but it is especially popular in Israel. It is usually quite spicy, therefore the name Eggs in Purgatory, and most often made in a cast-iron frying pan. You can adjust the heat by lowering the amount of fresh chilli and crushed chilli flakes you use. Or, you can eliminate them altogether if you want your eggs to be more heavenly.

2 tablespoons extra virgin olive oil

1 medium onion, peeled and finely diced

1 teaspoon finely chopped garlic

1 red pepper, cored, seeded, and finely diced

1 hot green or red chilli, stemmed, seeded, membrane removed, and finely chopped, or to taste

1 liter (1¾ pints) tomato sauce

2 tablespoons tomato purée

1 teaspoon ground cumin

½ teaspoon crushed chilli flakes

Salt and pepper

5 extra large eggs

2 tablespoons chopped flat-leaf parsley

Preheat the oven to 180ºC/350ºF/Gas Mark 4.

Heat the oil in a large heavy ovenproof frying pan over medium heat. Add the onion and garlic and cook, stirring often, for 5 minutes. Stir in the pepper and chilli and continue to cook, stirring frequently, for about 10 minutes or until the vegetables are soft and aromatic.

Stir in the tomato sauce and tomato purée along with the cumin and crushed chillies. Season with salt and pepper to taste and cook, stirring frequently, for about 10 minutes or just until the sauce begins to reduce slightly. (You can make the sauce and store it, covered and refrigerated. Reheat and proceed with making the final dish. In this way, you can cook 1 or 2 eggs at a time, rather than the entire number.)

Crack one egg at a time into a small cup. Carefully lay each egg into the simmering sauce in even spacing, slightly in from the edge of the pan. Place the final egg in the center.

Transfer to the preheated oven and bake for about 12 minutes or just until the whites are set and the yolks still runny.

Remove from the oven and sprinkle with parsley. Take the pan directly to the table and allow diners to serve themselves, taking one egg each.

Nutritional Analysis per Serving: calories 254, carbohydrates 25 g, fiber 6 g, protein 12 g, fat 14 g, sodium 284 mg, sugar 14 g.

WILD MUSHROOM GRATIN

Serves 4

Although this gratin stands alone nicely, it also makes a terrific side dish for a roast – either poultry or beef. If you can't find a mix of wild mushrooms, use white button mushrooms combined with chestnut mushrooms; the latter will add a little deeper color and flavor to the relatively bland buttons.

1 tablespoon walnut oil

10 g (¼ oz) unsalted butter

2 shallots, peeled and finely chopped

800 g (1 lb 12 oz) wild mushrooms, cleaned, stems removed, and sliced

1 teaspoon dried fines herbes

Salt and white pepper

2 tablespoons almond meal

125 ml (4 fl oz) double cream

Freshly grated nutmeg

55 g (2 oz) Gruyère cheese, grated

Preheat the oven to 180ºC/350ºF/Gas Mark 4.

Lightly butter a shallow 1-liter (1¾-pint) baking dish. Set aside.

Combine the oil and butter in a large sauté pan over medium heat. Add the shallots and cook, stirring occasionally, for about 3 minutes or until just translucent. Add the mushrooms and fines herbes and cook, stirring frequently, for about 5 minutes or until the mushrooms have begun to exude their liquid and soften. Season with salt and pepper to taste. Add the almond meal, stirring to blend, and cook for an additional couple of minutes to allow the meal to blend into the mushrooms.

Remove from the heat, stir in the cream, and season with nutmeg and, if necessary, additional salt and pepper. Pour the mixture into the prepared baking dish and sprinkle the top with the cheese. Place in the preheated oven and bake for about 12 minutes or until the edges are bubbling and the cheese is golden brown.

Remove from the oven and serve.

Nutritional Analysis per Serving: calories 359, carbohydrates 16 g, fiber 5 g, protein 16 g, fat 28 g, sodium 386 mg, sugar 4 g.

CHEESE SOUFFLÉ

Serves 2

Most soufflés have a mixture of flour and milk to give them some binding as they rise, but this one pops right up without it. However, it does fall mighty fast so have your fork ready as soon as it comes out of the oven. Interestingly, the nuttiness of the almond milk makes a great mate for the equally nutty Gruyère.

15 g (½ oz) salted butter, at room temperature, to grease ramekins

2 tablespoons grated Parmesan cheese

4 large eggs

50 ml (2 fl oz) sour cream

40 ml (1½ fl oz) unsweetened almond milk

½ teaspoon mustard powder

Salt and pepper

55 g (2 oz) Gruyère cheese, grated

Generously coat the interior of two 475-ml (16-fl oz) ramekins with butter. Add enough Parmesan cheese to completely coat the interior. Transfer to the refrigerator until ready to use.

Preheat the oven to 200ºC/400ºF/Gas Mark 6.

Combine the eggs, sour cream, almond milk, mustard, and salt and pepper to taste in a blender, processing until very light and airy.

Remove the ramekins from the refrigerator and place an equal amount of the Gruyère in the bottom of each one. Pour an equal portion of the egg mixture into each ramekin and carefully transfer to the preheated oven.

Bake for about 40 minutes or until golden brown and puffed up over the edge of the ramekin.

Remove from the oven and serve immediately as the soufflés will begin falling as soon as they are out of the oven.

Nutritional Analysis per Serving: calories 507, carbohydrates 4 g, fiber 0 g, protein 32 g, fat 40 g, sodium 672 mg, sugar 0 g.

FALAFEL WITH TAHINI SAUCE

Serves 4

Falafel is a Middle Eastern snack or street food, usually served in a pita pocket. It is so tasty on its own that I don't think it needs anything more than a drizzle of tahini to make it the perfect lunch dish, particularly if you combine it with a few tomato slices or some crunchy lettuce leaves.

When frying, make sure you have the oil deep enough to cover the cakes so that they brown quickly and easily.

Since this dish is relatively high in carbohydrates, take care about the remainder of your total carbohydrate intake for the day.

125 g (4½ oz) dried chickpeas

1 small shallot, peeled and chopped

115 g (4 oz) onions, peeled and chopped

15 g (½ oz) coriander leaves

1 teaspoon finely chopped garlic

½ teaspoon ground toasted cumin

¼ teaspoon ground allspice

¼ teaspoon paprika

¼ teaspoon black pepper

¼ teaspoon cayenne pepper or to taste

½ teaspoon bicarbonate of soda

Salt

Extra virgin olive oil for frying

125 ml (4 fl oz) Tahini Sauce (recipe follows)

Place the chickpeas in cold water to cover and soak for at least 8 hours or overnight.

Drain the chickpeas and rinse well under cold running water. Place in a blender and process to just chop. Add the shallot, onion, coriander, garlic, cumin, allspice, paprika, pepper, and cayenne and process to an almost smooth paste. If your blender isn't powerful enough to do the whole amount, process in batches to ensure a smooth mixture.

Scrape into a mixing bowl and add the bicarbonate of soda and salt, stirring to blend well.

Using your hands, form the mixture into cakes about 6 cm (2½ inches) in diameter. You should have about 8 small cakes. Don't make them too fat or the center will not cook when fried.

Heat the oil in a large frying pan (or if you have one, a deep-fat fryer) over medium heat. It should be deep enough to cover the cakes. When hot, but not smoking, add the chickpea cakes, a few at a time, and fry, turning once, for about 4 minutes or until both sides are golden and the cakes are cooked through.

Using a slotted spoon transfer to a double layer of kitchen paper to drain.

Serve immediately, 2 per person, drizzled with 2 tablespoons Tahini Sauce.

Nutritional Analysis per Serving (includes 2 tablespoons tahini sauce): calories 455, carbohydrates 35 g, fiber 8 g, protein 13g, fat 32 g, sodium 466 mg, sugar 6 g.

TAHINI SAUCE

Makes about 125 ml (4 fl oz)

4 tablespoons tahini (sesame seed paste)
Juice of ½ lemon
2½ tablespoons cool water

½ tablespoon finely chopped coriander

½ teaspoon finely chopped garlic

Pinch ground toasted cumin

Salt

Place the tahini in a small mixing bowl and gradually whisk in the lemon juice. The tahini will seize up a bit. Then, begin adding the water, whisking until you have the consistency of creamy yogurt. Again, the mix might seize a bit before it loosens.

Stir in the coriander, garlic, cumin, and salt.

Serve immediately or store, covered and refrigerated, until ready to use or for up to 5 days.

NOTE Tahini Sauce is outstanding on grilled fish.

Nutritional Analysis per Serving (2 tablespoons): calories 183, carbohydrates 8 g, fiber 2 g, protein 5 g, fat 16 g, sodium 301 mg, sugar 0 g.

SPICY CHICKEN BURGERS WITH GUACAMOLE

Serves 4

Kind of like a taco in flavor, these chicken burgers are zesty with Mexican seasonings and the guacamole adds just the right amount of buttery smoothness to complete the package. The guacamole makes a bit more than you will need to top the burgers, but it is so tasty an extra helping will be appreciated. I think you'll find that you won't miss the bun one bit!

450 g (1 lb) minced chicken

1 large egg white

1 jalapeño or other hot green chilli, stemmed, seeded, and finely chopped, or to taste

3 tablespoons finely chopped red pepper

2 tablespoons finely chopped spring onion

1 teaspoon chilli powder

¹/₄ teaspoon ground cumin

Salt and pepper

250 ml (8 fl oz) Guacamole (recipe follows)

Preheat the grill and oil the grill pan. Alternately, fry the burgers in a ridged griddle pan or a heavy-bottom frying pan.

Combine the chicken with the egg white, using your hands to blend. Add the chilli, red pepper, spring onion, chilli powder, and cumin. Again, using your hands, mix well to blend. Season with salt and pepper to taste and form the mix into 4 patties of equal size.

Place the burgers under the grill and grill for 5 minutes. Turn and grill for another 4 minutes for well-done.

Remove from the grill and serve topped with about 4 tablespoons Guacamole.

Nutritional Analysis per Serving (includes 4 tablespoons guacamole): calories 309, carbohydrates 6 g, fiber 4 g, protein 29 g, fat 20 g, sodium 322 mg, sugar 1 g.

GUACAMOLE

Makes about 500 ml (17 fl oz)

2 medium avocados, peeled, pitted, and mashed

Juice of 1 lime

50 g (1³/₄ oz) tomatoes, chopped

2 tablespoons chopped coriander

2 tablespoons chopped spring onion

1 teaspoon finely chopped hot green chilli or to taste

Salt and pepper

Combine the avocado with the lime juice, tomatoes, coriander, spring onion, and chilli. Season with salt and pepper to taste and serve.

Nutritional Analysis per Serving (4 tablespoons): calories 86, carbohydrates 6 g, fiber 4 g, protein 1 g, fat 7 g, sodium 78 mg, sugar 1 g.

ALMOND-CRUSTED CHICKEN STRIPS

Serves 4 (makes about 12 pieces)

This is a healthy version of those ubiquitous chicken fingers found in every chain restaurant. I like to dip them in a variety of sauces, but they are also delicious as is with a sprinkle of lemon juice to cut the richness. The nut coating adds a very special crunch that doesn't get soggy as a breaded coating often will. You can use pecans, walnuts, or pistachios in place of the almonds.

140 g (5 oz) unblanched almonds

1 teaspoon dried Italian or pizza herb mix

1/4 teaspoon smoked paprika

115 g (4 oz) Parmesan cheese, grated

Salt and pepper

2 large egg whites

450 g (1 lb) chicken strips

Extra virgin olive oil for drizzling, optional

Lemon wedges for serving

Preheat the oven to 190ºC/375ºF/Gas Mark 5.

Line a baking sheet with parchment paper or a nonstick silicone liner. Set aside.

Combine the almonds with the herb mix and paprika in the bowl of a food processor fitted with a metal blade. Process, using quick on and off turns, until the consistency of breadcrumbs is reached. Watch carefully as you do not want to pulverize the nuts.

Combine the nut mixture with the cheese in a large shallow bowl, stirring to blend completely. Season with salt and pepper to taste.

Place the egg whites in another large shallow bowl and whisk until very light and frothy.

Working with one piece at a time, dip the chicken pieces into the egg white and then roll in the nut mixture, taking care to evenly coat all sides. As coated, place on the prepared baking sheet.

When all of the chicken has been coated, drizzle each piece with a bit of olive oil, if using. Transfer to the preheated oven and bake for about 15 minutes or until golden brown and cooked through.

Remove from the oven and serve with lemon wedges.

Nutritional Analysis per Serving (3 pieces): calories 501, carbohydrates 6 g, fiber 3 g, protein 43 g, fat 33 g, sodium 645 mg, sugar 1 g.

THE BEST BEEF 'N' CHEESE BURGERS

Serves 4

What, another burger? Yes, indeed, and this one has to be made with grass-fed beef, which has great omega-3 content and gives you the added strength of disease-fighting conjugated linoleic acid (see my book *Grain Brain*, pages 140-141). When you put that chunk of cheese in the center you will score a 10 on the *Grain Brain* chart.

450 g (1 lb) coarsely minced beef

55 g (2 oz) onion, peeled and finely chopped

2 tablespoons iced water

Salt and pepper

4 x 4-cm (1½-inch) cubes Cheddar cheese

Place the beef in a medium bowl. Add the onion and iced water and season with salt and pepper to taste. Using your hands, gently mix to blend well.

Form the beef into 4 equal mounds. Place a cube of cheese in the center of each mound and then form the beef up and around the cheese. Shape each mound into a patty of equal size as you want them to cook evenly.

Preheat a nonstick ridged griddle pan over medium-high heat. When very hot, add the patties and grill, turning once, for about 4 minutes or until crusty and nicely browned. Turn and grill the remaining side for about 4 minutes or until brown and crusty and the burger is medium-rare – unless you prefer it well-done, which will require about 4 additional minutes of cooking.

Remove from the pan and serve with condiments, sliced tomato, and/or lettuce leaves.

Nutritional Analysis per Serving: calories 199, carbohydrates 2 g, fiber 0 g, protein 25 g, fat 10 g, sodium 433 mg, sugar 0 g.

GARLIC-HERB MUSSELS

Serves 4

Mussels are a picnic to cook and, in this recipe, the broth is as satisfying as the shellfish, so you have a two-for-one meal. Served with a tossed green salad, mussels make the perfect light lunch dish. You can add as much garlic and crushed chillies as your palate can stand – I've gone easy here, but feel free to fire up the pot.

4 tablespoons extra virgin olive oil

125 ml (4 fl oz) clam juice

Juice of ½ lemon

1 tablespoon finely chopped garlic

1 tablespoon chopped basil

1 teaspoon thyme leaves

Crushed chilli flakes

1.8 kg (4 lb) mussels, scrubbed clean, beards removed

40 g (1½ oz) butter, at room temperature

4 tablespoons chopped flat-leaf parsley

Heat the oil in a large, deep sauté pan over medium heat. When hot, add the clam and lemon juices along with the garlic, basil, thyme, and crushed chillies. Bring to a boil and immediately add the mussels. Cover and cook for about 6 minutes or until all of the mussels have opened. Swirl in the butter and when melted, ladle into a shallow tureen. Serve with the broth and parsley sprinkled over the top.

VARIATION 225 g (8 oz) of chopped chorizo or other spicy sausage can be added with the mussels.

Nutritional Analysis per Serving: calories 528, carbohydrates 16 g, fiber 0 g, protein 46 g, fat 31 g, sodium 766 mg, sugar 0 g.

MAIN MEALS

The one *Grain Brain* diet caveat that many cooks find difficult is the elimination of grains and starches on the dinner plate. However, with the variety of delectable dishes in this section I believe you will very quickly forget about potatoes, bread, and pasta. I have listed vegetable dishes first as I encourage you to think of vegetables as the center of the plate with proteins as the accompaniment, but we do have a few non-meat main courses also. In all cases, please remember that I advocate organically grown produce, extra virgin oil, organic unsalted butter, grass-fed, pasture-raised meats, and wild, line-caught (when appropriate) fish.

VEGETABLES

Caponata
Roasted Mixed Vegetables
Southwest Vegetable Sauté
Healthy Green Slaw
Roasted Broccoli with Garlic
Broccoli, Mushrooms, and Feta
Broccoli in Coconut Sauce
Brussels Sprouts with Pancetta and Sage
Sautéed Greens
Chard Tagine
Spinach with Spring Onions and Pumpkin Seeds

Grilled Radicchio

Cabbage and Onion Braise

Asparagus with Walnut Aïoli

Grilled Asparagus and Salad Onions

Grilled Sweet and Sour Beetroot

Radishes Braised in Butter

Braised Baby Artichokes

Grilled Parmesan Tomatoes

Sautéed Cherry Tomatoes and Herbs

Fried Green Plantains (Tostones)

Butternut Squash with Spinach and Pistachios

Courgette Casserole with Prosciutto and Cheese

Celery and Fennel with Anchovy Sauce

Kohlrabi Gratin

Cauliflower with Lemon-Parsley Butter

Cauliflower "Couscous"

Sesame-Scented Green and Yellow Beans

Green Beans with Walnuts

CAPONATA

Makes about 16 servings

Although caponata can be eaten immediately, it is best after it rests for a day. This gives the flavors a chance to mellow. It keeps very well and is terrific to have on hand for snacking, to use as a main meal, or in a salad. When seasoning, if you are adding capers, remember that they are going to add some salt to the mix.

75 ml (3 fl oz) extra virgin olive oil

450 g (1 lb) red onions, diced

2 teaspoons finely chopped garlic

900 g (2 lb) aubergines, trimmed and cut into cubes

2 large red or green peppers, cored, seeded, membrane removed, and diced

750 ml (1¼ pints) canned diced tomatoes including their juice

140 g (5 oz) green olives, chopped

1 tablespoon chopped basil

1 teaspoon chopped oregano

175 ml (6 fl oz) red wine vinegar

4 tablespoons capers, optional

Heat the oil in a large nonstick frying pan over medium heat. Add the onions and garlic and cook, stirring frequently, for 5 minutes. Add the aubergines and continue to cook, stirring, for 10 minutes or just until the aubergine softens.

Stir in the peppers, tomatoes, olives, basil, and oregano. Cook for an additional 5 minutes or just until the vegetables have softened a bit. Stir in the vinegar, season with salt and pepper to taste, and bring to a boil.

Remove from the heat, stir in the capers, if using, and set aside to cool.

Serve at room temperature.

VARIATION One large chopped courgette may be added with the other vegetables as can 75 g (2³/₄ oz) pine nuts along with the capers.

Nutritional Analysis per Serving (125 ml/4 fl oz): calories 92, carbohydrates 10 g, fiber 2 g, protein 1 g, fat 6 g, sodium 237 mg, sugar 4 g.

ROASTED MIXED VEGETABLES

Serves 6

Roasted vegetables are fantastic to have on hand as they can be eaten as is or with some shaved hard cheese for lunch or a snack, or on a platter with grilled meat or fish. They keep very well, covered and refrigerated, for up to a week or so. You can make as many or as few as you like and make any combination that appeals to you. You can grill these, too – the smokiness of the grill adds a whole new dimension to the flavor. You can also eliminate the vinegar if you prefer the more subtle flavor of olive oil.

2 portobello mushroom caps, cleaned

2 courgettes, trimmed and cut, crosswise, into 1-cm (¹/₂-inch) thick slices

1 red pepper, cored, seeded, membrane removed, and cut, lengthwise, into sixths

225 g (8 oz) asparagus, tough ends removed

1 small aubergine, trimmed and cut, crosswise, into 1-cm (¹/₂-inch) thick slices

175 ml (6 fl oz) extra virgin olive oil

125 ml (4 fl oz) balsamic vinegar

2 teaspoons rosemary

Salt and pepper

Preheat the oven to 190ºC/375ºF/Gas Mark 5.

Place the mushrooms, courgettes, peppers, asparagus, and aubergine in a large, rimmed baking dish. Add the olive oil, vinegar, rosemary, and salt and pepper, tossing to coat well.

Place in the preheated oven and roast, turning occasionally, for about 15 minutes or until the vegetables are nicely colored, but still crisp-tender.

VARIATION For a Southwestern flavor, replace the rosemary with 1 tablespoon chilli powder, $1/2$ teaspoon ground cumin, and $1/4$ teaspoon cayenne pepper.

Nutritional Analysis per Serving: calories 298, carbohydrates 13 g, fiber 3 g, protein 3 g, fat 29 g, sodium 214 mg, sugar 8 g.

SOUTHWEST VEGETABLE SAUTÉ

Serves 4

Rather like a Chinese vegetable stir-fry without the soy sauce and ginger, these vegetables look beautiful on the plate and make a light dinner with a side of guacamole and jack (or Cheddar) cheese or partnered with grilled meats or fish.

40 g ($1^1/_2$ oz) butter

1 chayote seeded and cut into matchsticks

1 red pepper, stemmed, seeded, membrane removed, and cut into matchsticks

1 carrot, peeled and cut into matchsticks

1 red onion, peeled and cut, lengthwise, into strips

1 small jicama, peeled and cut into matchsticks

1 teaspoon ground cumin

Salt and pepper

4 tablespoons chopped coriander

Heat the butter in a large frying pan over medium heat. Add the chayote, red pepper, carrot, red onion, and jicama. Season with cumin, salt and pepper and cook, tossing and turning with tongs, for about 3 minutes or just until crisp-tender.

Remove from the heat and toss in the coriander. Serve immediately before the hot vegetables have a chance to wilt further.

Nutritional Analysis per Serving: calories 142, carbohydrates 15 g, fiber 6 g, protein 2 g, fat 9 g, sodium 162 mg, sugar 5 g.

NOTE: Chayote, known also as christophene, is a gourd-like vegetable, comparable to a squash. They can be found in Asian stores, but if unavailable pattypan squash or courgette could be used instead. Jicama is a bulbous root vegetable with white crunchy flesh, popular in Mexican cooking. Water chestnuts or white radish (mooli) could be substituted.

HEALTHY GREEN SLAW

Serves 4

We usually think of slaw as being a cold salad for summer barbecues and picnics. This slaw resembles a summer coleslaw, but because it is quickly tossed in a wok, although the vegetables remain crisp and lively, the salad is warm.

2 tablespoons avocado oil
1 small Savoy cabbage, cored and cut into slivers
1 bunch kale, tough stems removed and cut into slivers
Florets from 1 bunch broccoli, stalks peeled and cut into slivers
Salt and pepper
65 g (2¼ oz) sunflower seeds

Heat the oil in a wok over medium-high heat. Add the cabbage, kale, and broccoli. Season with salt and pepper to taste and stir-fry, tossing and turning, for about 5 minutes or until all of the vegetables are just barely cooked. Add the sunflower seeds, tossing to blend.

Remove from the heat and serve.

Nutritional Analysis per Serving: calories 26, carbohydrates 24 g, fiber 9 g, protein 12 g, fat 17 g, sodium 242 mg, sugar 5 g.

ROASTED BROCCOLI WITH GARLIC

Serves 4

This is one of my favorite ways to cook broccoli; a bit charred around the edges and redolent with garlic. It is not difficult to do and the dish works well with almost any protein. With a crumble of ricotta salata or a chunk of cheese melting over the top, it becomes a filling main course on its own.

1 bunch broccoli

2 tablespoons finely chopped garlic

Salt and crushed chilli flakes

4 tablespoons extra virgin olive oil

Preheat the oven to 190ºC/375ºF/Gas Mark 5.

Using a vegetable peeler, trim the outer skin from the broccoli stalks. Split each stalk including the florets into 2 or 3 pieces of fairly equal size. Place the stalks on a roasting tray. Sprinkle the garlic, salt, and crushed chillies over the top. Pour on the olive oil and toss to evenly coat each piece of broccoli.

Transfer to the preheated oven and roast, turning occasionally, for about 15 minutes or until just barely tender and slightly charred on the edges.

Remove from the oven and serve hot or at room temperature.

Nutritional Analysis per Serving: calories 221, carbohydrates 21 g, fiber 9 g, protein 7 g, fat 15 g, sodium 256 mg, sugar 4 g.

BROCCOLI, MUSHROOMS, AND FETA

Serves 4

If you add a bit more feta to this recipe, it can stand alone on the plate. If you do, be sure to buy a beautiful imported sheep's milk feta. This recipe only uses the broccoli florets, but be sure to save the stems. They can be peeled, cut into pieces, and sautéed or shaved into salads.

2 tablespoons walnut oil

55 g (2 oz) shallots, finely diced

225 g (8 oz) chestnut mushrooms, trimmed and sliced

1 bunch broccoli, cut into florets

Salt and pepper

115 g (4 oz) feta cheese, crumbled

Heat the walnut oil in a large frying pan over medium heat. Add the shallots and cook, stirring frequently, for about 2 minutes or just until softened. Add the mushrooms and continue to cook, stirring frequently, for about 5 minutes or just until the mushrooms have begun to exude their liquid. Add the broccoli and season with salt and pepper to taste. Cook, tossing and turning with tongs, for about 10 minutes or until the broccoli is crisp-tender.

Add the feta, cover, and remove from the heat. Let rest for about 2 minutes or just until the feta begins to melt.

Remove from the heat and serve immediately.

Nutritional Analysis per Serving: calories 259, carbohydrates 24 g, fiber 10 g, protein 13 g, fat 15 g, sodium 465 mg, sugar 6 g.

BROCCOLI IN COCONUT SAUCE

Serves 4

This is certainly a different broccoli from the plain old green that has been so maligned over the years. The tahini and coconut add totally unexpected flavor and take the broccoli from the cafeteria table to the healthy, "can I have seconds" one.

3 cloves garlic

1 hot green chilli or to taste

3 tablespoons unsweetened coconut

1 tablespoon tahini

1 tablespoon extra virgin olive oil

1 bunch broccoli, cut into florets

Salt

Preheat the oven to 180ºC/350ºF/Gas Mark 4.

Line a roasting tray with parchment paper. Set aside.

Combine the garlic, chilli, coconut, tahini, and olive oil in a food processor or blender and process until finely chopped.

Place the broccoli in a mixing bowl, add the coconut mixture and salt, and toss to coat.

Lay the broccoli out on the prepared roasting tray in a single layer. Transfer to the preheated oven and roast for about 15 minutes or just until barely tender and lightly colored.

Remove from the oven and serve.

Nutritional Analysis per Serving: calories 195, carbohydrates 21 g, fiber 9 g, protein 7 g, fat 11 g, sodium 260 mg, sugar 4 g.

BRUSSELS SPROUTS WITH PANCETTA AND SAGE

Serves 4

When I was a child no one ate Brussels sprouts; they were boiled to an unappetizing gray color and were soggy and tasteless. But I've noticed that they have recently gained in popularity, even in 4-star restaurants. This is probably because nowadays, they are most often roasted to bring out their inherent sweetness. Here, the salty pancetta and aromatic sage deepen the sweetness and make them particularly inviting.

675 g (1 lb 8 oz) Brussels sprouts, trimmed and halved

225 g (8 oz) pancetta, cut into small cubes

1 tablespoon chopped sage

1 tablespoon freshly grated orange zest

2 tablespoons extra virgin olive oil

Pepper

Preheat the oven to 200ºC/400ºF/Gas Mark 6.

Combine the Brussels sprouts with the pancetta, sage, and orange zest on a roasting tray. Add the olive oil, tossing to coat well and evenly distribute all of the ingredients. Season with pepper to taste and transfer to the preheated oven. Roast, turning a couple of times, for about 20 minutes or until the Brussels sprouts are tender and the pancetta is crisp.

Remove from the oven and serve.

NOTE For those on a restricted sodium diet, the pancetta can be eliminated from the recipe or replaced with 115 g (4 oz) low-sodium bacon.

Nutritional Analysis per Serving: calories 348, carbohydrates 16 g, fiber 5 g, protein 13 g, fat 26 g, sodium 939 mg, sugar 3 g.

SAUTÉED GREENS

Serves 4

This is the basic method for sautéing all types of greens – spring, kale, beet leaves, escarole, endive, chard – well, you get it, any type of green you can find. To the basic recipe you can add a handful of pine nuts or toasted flaked almonds, a good dose of freshly grated orange or lemon zest, a chopped raw red or white onion, a bunch of chopped spring onions, green part included, finely chopped green or red hot chilli, or any fresh herb that you favor. I make them my own by tossing in 3 tablespoons of butter just before I take them off the stove and then shaving Parmesan cheese over the top.

Please do be mindful that that huge mound of chopped raw greens will cook down to a very manageable amount, so always start with much more than you think you need.

3 tablespoons extra virgin olive oil

1 teaspoon finely chopped garlic

2 bunches fresh greens, well washed and chopped

Crushed chilli flakes

Salt

Heat the oil in a large frying pan with a lid over medium heat. Add the garlic and cook, stirring, for 2 minutes. Add the greens (they will more than fill the pan) and season with chilli flakes and salt. Add 4 tablespoons water, cover, and cook for about 3 minutes or just until the greens have wilted enough for you to be able to toss them.

Uncover and, using tongs, toss the greens to blend the cooked ones into those that are still raw. Cover and cook for an additional 4 minutes or until the greens are just tender, but not overcooked and soggy.

Remove from the heat and serve.

Nutritional Analysis per Serving: calories 160, carbohydrates 13 g, fiber 3 g, protein 6 g, fat 12 g, sodium 343 mg, sugar 0 g.

CHARD TAGINE

Serves 4

A tagine is a Moroccan stew scented with spices that is often served with couscous. For a double *Grain Brain* hit, you might serve this particular stew with Cauliflower Couscous (see page 133) and you'll have a memorable all-vegetable meal.

2 bunches rainbow chard, chopped

4 tablespoons extra virgin olive oil

1 shallot, peeled and finely chopped

225 g (8 oz) red onions, peeled and chopped

1½ teaspoons paprika

½ teaspoon ground coriander

¼ teaspoon ground cinnamon

Salt and pepper

4 tablespoons chopped coriander

4 tablespoons chopped flat-leaf parsley

1 tablespoon flaxseeds

1 teaspoon lemon juice

Wash the chard well in cold running water. Place in a colander to drain, but do not dry.

Heat the oil in a large frying pan over medium heat. Add the shallot and onions along with the paprika, ground coriander, and cinnamon. Cook, stirring occasionally, for about 10 minutes or until the onion is very soft.

Add the reserved chard and season with salt and pepper to taste. Cover, keeping the lid askew, and cook, stirring occasionally, for about 5 minutes or until the chard is tender.

Remove from the heat, stir in the chopped coriander, parsley, flaxseeds, and lemon juice, and serve.

Nutritional Analysis per Serving: calories 256, carbohydrates 16 g, fiber 6 g, protein 6 g, fat 21 g, sodium 635 mg, sugar 5 g.

SPINACH WITH SPRING ONIONS AND PUMPKIN SEEDS

Serves 4

The pumpkin seeds and spring onions add a little crunch and snap to the wilted spinach. You could also use toasted pine nuts, chopped walnuts, or cashews in place of the pumpkin seeds.

450 g (1 lb) spinach, tough stems removed

1 tablespoon avocado oil

Salt and cracked black pepper

4 tablespoons toasted pumpkin seeds

4 tablespoons chopped spring onions, including some green part

Wash the spinach well. Using a salad spinner, spin to dry slightly. You want to have some droplets of water clinging to the leaves.

Heat the oil in a large frying pan over medium heat. Add the spinach, season with salt and pepper to taste and, using tongs, toss and turn to just wilt. This shouldn't take more than a minute.

Toss in the pumpkin seeds and spring onions and serve immediately.

Nutritional Analysis per Serving: calories 93, carbohydrates 5 g, fiber 2 g, protein 5 g, fat 7 g, sodium 357 mg, sugar 0 g.

GRILLED RADICCHIO

Serves 4

Radicchio, like all chicories, can be quite bitter, but once it is grilled the flavor mellows. Just before it is finished grilling, I will often lay a couple of slices of soft cheese on the top and let it melt a bit into the radicchio, rather than shave Parmesan on after it has cooked. This dish can add a bit of pizzazz to grilled meats, poultry, or fish.

4 heads radicchio, trimmed and cut, lengthwise, in half

4 tablespoons extra virgin olive oil

4 tablespoons balsamic vinegar

Salt and pepper

Parmesan cheese for shaving, optional

Lay the radicchio halves, cut side up, in a baking dish. Combine the oil and vinegar and drizzle it over the top of each piece. Set aside to marinate for 30 minutes.

Preheat the grill and oil the grill pan or alternatively oil a ridged griddle pan over high heat.

Season the radicchio with salt and pepper. Place, cut side up, under the preheated grill (or in the hot pan) and grill, turning occasionally, for about 10 minutes or until lightly colored and cooked through.

Using tongs, transfer the radicchio to a serving platter. Let cool just a bit and then, if using, shave Parmesan over the top and serve.

Nutritional Analysis per Serving: calories 128, carbohydrates 2 g, fiber 0 g, protein 0 g, fat 14 g, sodium 152 mg, sugar 2 g.

CABBAGE AND ONION BRAISE

Serves 4

Braising takes the bite out of cabbage and the wine makes a lovely flavorful broth. This is a recipe you can truly make your own by changing the spices and adding herbs and/or chillies or a touch of citrus. You don't absolutely have to add the stevia, but it does help pull out the sweetness of cabbage.

55 g (2 oz) butter

1 medium head green cabbage, cored and shredded

1 large onion, peeled and pulled into rings

1 red pepper, cored, seeded, and cut into fine dice

1 green pepper, cored, seeded, and cut, lengthwise, into strips

1 teaspoon stevia

1 teaspoon caraway seeds

Salt and pepper

4 tablespoons dry white wine

Preheat the oven to 180ºC/350ºF/Gas Mark 4.

Melt the butter in a large heavy-bottom ovenproof saucepan over medium heat. Add the cabbage, onion, and peppers, tossing to blend. Sprinkle on the stevia and caraway seeds and season with salt and pepper to taste. Add the white wine and again toss to blend.

Cover and transfer to the preheated oven. Cook, covered, for about 30 minutes or until the vegetables are very tender and well flavored.

Remove from the oven and serve.

Nutritional Analysis per Serving: calories 171, carbohydrates 13 g, fiber 5 g, protein 3 g, fat 11 g, sodium 174 mg, sugar 6 g.

ASPARAGUS WITH WALNUT AÏOLI

Serves 4

Aïoli is a garlic-based sauce from the Provence region of France. It is traditionally served as a sauce for steamed vegetables, fish, or hard-boiled eggs, but it can also be used as a garnish for fish stews. It can be flavored in many different ways, but this walnut version is one of my favorites. Although the recipe calls for asparagus, don't hesitate to use the sauce with other vegetables. It will keep, covered and refrigerated, for up to 3 days.

675 g (1 lb 8 oz) (about 30 spears) asparagus, trimmed of woody
ends

1 tablespoon extra virgin olive oil

Salt

125 ml (4 fl oz) Walnut Aïoli (recipe follows)

2 tablespoons chopped toasted walnuts, optional

Preheat the oven to 200ºC/400ºF/Gas Mark 6.

Lay the asparagus out on a roasting tray. Add the olive oil and salt
and toss to coat. Transfer to the preheated oven and roast for about
18 minutes or until still slightly crisp and showing just a hint of char.

Remove from the oven and place on a serving platter. Spoon the
aïoli over the top, sprinkle with toasted walnuts, if desired.

Nutritional Analysis per Serving: calories 266, carbohydrates 7 g, fiber 4 g,
protein 6 g, fat 26 g, sodium 184 mg, sugar 2 g.

WALNUT AÏOLI

Makes about 550 ml (19 fl oz)

4 large egg yolks, at room temperature

2 teaspoons roasted garlic purée (see Note)

3 tablespoons lemon juice

650 ml (1 pint) extra virgin olive oil

4 tablespoons walnut oil

75 g (2³/₄ oz) toasted walnuts, finely chopped

Salt and cayenne pepper

Combine the egg yolks with the garlic in the bowl of a food
processor fitted with a metal blade, and process to blend. With the
motor running, add the lemon juice. When the juice has blended,
begin to add the olive and walnut oils in a slow, steady stream. The
sauce should be quite thick and creamy.

Scrape the mixture into a clean bowl. Stir in the walnuts and season with salt and cayenne. Use immediately or store, covered and refrigerated, for up to 3 days.

NOTE You can purchase premade roast garlic, but please don't. Fresh homemade is a snap to do, a boon to have on hand, and better for you. To make roasted garlic purée, lay the unpeeled cloves from 3 heads of garlic (or as many as you want) on a piece of aluminium foil large enough to enclose them completely. Toss with about 2 table-spoons extra virgin olive oil. Fold the foil up and over the garlic and pinch together to seal tightly. Do not pile the cloves up; try to keep them in a single layer. Place in a baking dish in a preheated 180ºC/350ºF/Gas Mark 4 oven and bake for about 30 minutes or until very soft. Remove from the oven and allow to cool. When cool enough to handle, using your fingertips, push the soft garlic from the skins into a small bowl. Mash the cloves with a kitchen fork and, if not using immediately, transfer to a small glass container, cover and refrigerate for up to 1 week or freeze for up to 3 months.

Nutritional Analysis per Serving (125 ml/4 fl oz): calories 177, carbohydrates 0 g, fiber 0 g, protein 1 g, fat 20 g, sodium 17 mg, sugar 0 g.

GRILLED ASPARAGUS AND SALAD ONIONS

Serves 6

This dish is perfect in the spring when both asparagus and new, almost-sweet onions are in their prime.

450 g (1 lb) asparagus, trimmed of woody ends

450 g (1 lb) salad onions, trimmed

250 ml (8 fl oz) extra virgin olive oil

Salt and pepper

2¹/₂ tablespoons champagne vinegar

1¹/₂ tablespoons Dijon mustard

Preheat the grill and oil the grill pan. Alternatively, preheat the oven to 200ºC/400ºF/Gas Mark 6.

Combine the asparagus and onions in a baking dish. Add 4 tablespoons of the oil along with salt and pepper to taste, tossing to coat well.

Place the vegetables under the preheated grill and grill, turning frequently, for about 8 minutes or until crisp-tender and nicely caramelized. If roasting, place on a nonstick roasting tray and roast in the preheated oven for about the same amount of time.

While the vegetables are grilling, make the dressing.

Combine the vinegar and mustard in a small mixing bowl, whisking to combine. Whisk in the remaining olive oil, beating to emulsify. Season with salt and pepper to taste.

Remove the vegetables from the grill or oven and place on a serving platter. Drizzle the dressing over the top and serve.

Nutritional Analysis per Serving: calories 365, carbohydrates 10 g, fiber 3 g, protein 3 g, fat 38 g, sodium 209 mg, sugar 3 g.

GRILLED SWEET AND SOUR BEETROOT

Serves 6

I guarantee that people who don't like beetroot will love this recipe. There is now such a wide variety of beetroot available that you can make this dish into a rainbow of colors and sizes. I have seen white, candy cane, yellow, purple, Chioggia, baby and so it goes. The best thing about beetroot is that their leaves are as useful and delicious as the root, so make sure that you ask that the leaves be kept on when purchasing.

4 tablespoons extra virgin olive oil

4 tablespoons balsamic vinegar

1 tablespoon red wine vinegar

1 tablespoon stevia

1 teaspoon finely chopped garlic

900 g (2 lb) cooked whole small beetroot or quartered large
beetroot

Salt and pepper

Combine the oil with the vinegars in a large bowl, whisking to blend. Add the stevia and garlic, whisking to incorporate. Set aside, whisking occasionally, until the flavors blend.

When blended, add the beetroot, tossing to coat. Season with salt and pepper to taste. Set aside, tossing occasionally, for 30 minutes.

Preheat the grill and oil the grill pan. Alternatively, preheat the oven to 190°C/375°F/Gas Mark 5.

Place the beetroot under the preheated grill and grill, turning occasionally, for about 5 minutes or until nicely glazed. If roasting, place the beetroot in a single layer on a roasting tray, place in the preheated oven, and roast for about 6 minutes or until nicely glazed.

Remove from the grill or oven and serve hot or at room temperature.

Nutritional Analysis per Serving: calories 157, carbohydrates 16 g, fiber 3 g, protein 2 g, fat 9 g, sodium 154 mg, sugar 13 g.

RADISHES BRAISED IN BUTTER

Serves 4

Most Americans think of radishes in a salad or as a garnish on a taco, but the French have been cooking them for generations; always braised in butter. They are an inexpensive vegetable with lots of flavor, and the butter softens their piquancy so they make a tasty dish alongside almost any protein. The leaves may also be used in salads or in a braise with other spicy greens; or, if you like, you can cut them into slivers and toss the raw leaves into the warm radishes just before serving.

2 bunches crisp red radishes

40 g (1½ oz) butter

75 ml (3 fl oz) Chicken Stock (see page 33) or low-sodium chicken
    stock or water

¼ teaspoon stevia

Salt and pepper

Trim the radishes, leaving just a bit of the stem. Scrub them well
as dirt can often cling around the stem and root end. If they have
stringy rootlets, pull off and discard.

Melt the butter over medium heat in a frying pan (with a lid) large
enough to hold the radishes in a single layer. Add the radishes, stock,
and stevia and season with salt and pepper to taste. Cover, lower the
heat, and braise for about 20 minutes or until easily pierced with the
point of a small sharp knife.

Remove from the heat and serve.

Nutritional Analysis per Serving: calories 109, carbohydrates 7 g, fiber 3 g,
protein 2 g, fat 9 g, sodium 230 mg, sugar 4 g.

BRAISED BABY ARTICHOKES

Serves 6

Although they are not easy to find, baby artichokes are a real delicacy.
Braised, they become very tender and quite unlike the large globe
artichokes whose flesh has to be pulled off the leaves with your teeth.
This recipe is almost a classic Italian take on a favorite Mediterranean
vegetable.

1 lemon

900 g (2 lb) baby artichokes

Approximately 75 ml (3 fl oz) extra virgin olive oil

2 shallots, peeled and finely chopped

2 cloves garlic, peeled and finely chopped

Freshly grated zest of 1 orange

125 ml (4 fl oz) dry white wine

Salt and pepper

Fill a large bowl with cold water. Cut the lemon in half and squeeze the juice into the water. Then, add the squeezed halves.

Working with one at a time, trim the top prickly tips from each artichoke. Lay the artichoke on its side and make one swift cut with a sharp knife to neatly trim about 5 mm ($1/4$ inch) off the top. If the artichokes have stems, using a vegetable peeler, peel off the tough outer skin and lop off the dry bottom. Pull off any damaged outer leaves and then cut each artichoke in half, lengthwise. Immediately place each cut artichoke into the lemon water to keep it from discoloring. Continue trimming until all of the artichokes are done.

Cover the bottom of a large sauté pan with about 4 tablespoons of the olive oil. Place over medium heat and add the shallots and garlic. Cook, stirring frequently, for about 2 minutes or just until softened.

Add the artichokes, cut side down. Add the orange zest and white wine and season with salt and pepper to taste. Cover and bring to a simmer. Lower the heat and simmer for about 20 minutes or until the artichokes are tender.

Remove from the heat and drizzle with the remaining extra virgin olive oil. Taste and, if necessary, season with additional salt and pepper. Serve warm or at room temperature. Or, cool and store, covered and refrigerated, for up to 1 week.

Nutritional Analysis per Serving: calories 117, carbohydrates 10 g, fiber 4 g, protein 2 g, fat 7 g, sodium 155 mg, sugar 2 g.

GRILLED PARMESAN TOMATOES

Serves 4

One tomato is usually enough for a serving, but these are so tasty we suggest you make a couple of extras as, if not eaten, they can be served at room temperature for lunch. The tomatoes can also be cooked entirely under a preheated grill, but do watch carefully to keep the cheese from burning.

4 large ripe but firm tomatoes

50 g (1¾ oz) Parmesan cheese, grated

1 tablespoon chopped basil leaves

25 g (1 oz) butter, melted

Salt and pepper

Preheat the grill and oil the grill pan or preheat the oven to 190ºC/375ºF/Gas Mark 5.

Cut each tomato in half, crosswise. Do not core.

Combine the cheese and basil in a small mixing bowl. Spoon equal portions of the mixture on the cut side of each tomato. Drizzle with melted butter and season with salt and pepper to taste.

Place the tomatoes, cut side up, under the preheated grill. Cover and grill for 3 minutes. Uncover and grill for another minute or so or until the top is bubbling. Alternatively, place the tomatoes on a baking sheet in the preheated oven and bake for about 10 minutes or until the top is bubbling. (If you want the tops to brown, preheat the grill and place the roasted tomatoes under the grill for 30 seconds or so.)

Remove from the grill and serve.

Nutritional Analysis per Serving: calories 131, carbohydrates 9 g, fiber 2 g, protein 5 g, fat 9 g, sodium 341 mg, sugar 5 g.

SAUTÉED CHERRY TOMATOES AND HERBS

Serves 4

This dish is lovely when done with cherry tomatoes of different sizes and colors. Even if they are tiny, cut them in half otherwise you'll get a good squirt of juice in the eye when you prick them with your fork. To change the flavor, substitute extra virgin olive oil for the butter.

75 g (2³/₄ oz) butter

900 g (2 lb) mixed cherry tomatoes, halved

Salt and pepper

2 tablespoons chopped flat-leaf parsley

2 tablespoons chopped chives

2 tablespoons chopped basil

Heat the butter in a large frying pan over medium heat. Add the tomatoes, season with salt and pepper to taste and cook, stirring occasionally, for about 4 minutes or until just barely soft and oozing their juices. Do not overcook or you will have mush.

Remove from the heat and stir in the parsley, chives, and basil. Taste and, if necessary, add additional salt.

Serve warm or at room temperature.

Nutritional Analysis per Serving: calories 162, carbohydrates 6 g, fiber 2 g, protein 2 g, fat 15 g, sodium 299 mg, sugar 4 g.

FRIED GREEN PLANTAINS (TOSTONES)

Serves 4

Plantains are not often found on most American tables, except on those of families from Caribbean or Latin American countries, where plantains are an everyday staple. One of the most popular ways to cook them is this one – fried until crisp and golden and called tostones. They also make an unsurpassed snack. You can substitute extra virgin olive oil or avocado oil for the coconut oil to fry.

2 green plantains

Coconut oil for frying

Salt

Place the oil in a medium saucepan over medium-high heat. Bring to 190ºC/375ºF on a sugar thermometer.

While the oil is heating, peel the plantains and cut them, cross-wise, into 1.5-cm (³/₄-inch) thick slices.

When the oil has reached temperature, begin frying the plantains. Do not crowd the pan. Fry for about 3 minutes or until just tender. Do not turn off the heat; maintain the temperature.

Lift the plantains from the oil and place on a double layer of kitchen paper to drain for 1 minute.

Using a kitchen fork, smash the warm slices into flattened rounds. Return to the hot oil and fry for another 4 minutes or until very crisp and golden brown. Continue frying until all of the plantains have been fried.

Generously sprinkle with salt and serve hot and crisp.

Nutritional Analysis per Serving: calories 229, carbohydrates 29 g, fiber 2 g, protein 1 g, fat 13 g, sodium 294 mg, sugar 13 g.

BUTTERNUT SQUASH WITH SPINACH AND PISTACHIOS

Serves 4

You can make this dish with any type of hard-skinned squash, including pumpkin. If you want to make it a main meal, add about 225 g (8 oz) of crumbled ricotta salata or feta cheese when the squash is still hot. The cheese will melt a bit and add some brininess to the sweet roasted squash.

900 g (2 lb) butternut squash, peeled and cut into large cubes (see Note)

40 g (1½ oz) ghee or butter, melted

2 tablespoons balsamic vinegar

1 teaspoon lemon juice

Salt and pepper

125 g (4½ oz) baby spinach or rocket or finely chopped greens of choice

55 g (2 oz) toasted unsalted pistachios

Preheat the oven to 180ºC/350ºF/Gas Mark 4.

Line a roasting tray with parchment paper. Set aside.

Combine the squash with the ghee, vinegar, and lemon juice in a large mixing bowl. Season with salt and pepper to taste and toss to coat well.

Spread the seasoned squash in a single layer on the prepared roasting tray. Transfer to the preheated oven and roast, turning occasionally, for about 25 minutes or until golden brown and tender.

Place the spinach in a large mixing bowl. Remove the squash from the oven and pour it over the spinach. Add the nuts and quickly toss to blend. Taste and, if necessary, season with additional salt and pepper.

Serve immediately.

NOTE Make sure that the squash cubes are of an equal size so that they roast evenly.

Nutritional Analysis per Serving: calories 248, carbohydrates 27 g, fiber 9 g, protein 5 g, fat 15 g, sodium 499 mg, sugar 6 g.

COURGETTE CASSEROLE WITH PROSCIUTTO AND CHEESE

Serves 4

This dish partners well with grilled meat or poultry since it is quite rich, but it can certainly stand alone as a filling lunch or brunch dish, or even, as a light supper.

2 tablespoons extra virgin olive oil

25 g (1 oz) butter

675 g (1 lb 8 oz) courgettes, trimmed and cut, crosswise, into
    5-mm (¼-inch) thick slices

4 large eggs, beaten

115 g (4 oz) Parma ham, chopped

4 tablespoons chopped sun-dried tomatoes

4 tablespoons grated Asiago or Parmesan cheese

Pepper

Preheat the oven to 200°C/400°F/Gas Mark 6.

Heat the oil and butter in a large cast-iron frying pan over medium heat. Add the courgettes and cook, stirring frequently, for about 5 minutes or just until beginning to soften and exude their liquid.

Combine the eggs with the Parma ham, sun-dried tomatoes, and cheese. Season with pepper and pour over the courgettes. Transfer to the preheated oven and bake for about 20 minutes or until the center is set and the top is golden brown.

Remove from the oven, cut into quarters, and serve.

Nutritional Analysis per Serving: calories 294, carbohydrates 9 g, fiber 2 g, protein 17 g, fat 22 g, sodium 712 mg, sugar 5 g.

CELERY AND FENNEL WITH ANCHOVY SAUCE

Serves 4

This dish is unusual in its flavor and in the combination of celery and fennel, two vegetables we usually eat raw. Don't forget to save some of the fennel fronds for garnish – they add a wonderful freshness to the warm vegetables.

125 ml (4 fl oz) Chicken Stock (see page 33) or low-sodium chicken stock

2 cloves garlic

1 bay leaf

1/4 teaspoon coriander seeds

1/4 teaspoon fennel seeds

2 anchovy fillets, drained and chopped

1 tablespoon extra virgin olive oil

1 tablespoon chopped flat-leaf parsley

1 teaspoon chopped capers, well-drained

1 teaspoon freshly grated orange zest

1/2 teaspoon red wine vinegar

Pepper

5 ribs celery, peeled and cut, on the diagonal, into 5-mm (1/4-inch) thick slices

2 bulbs fennel, trimmed, quartered lengthwise, and cut, on the diagonal, into 5-mm (1/4-inch) thick slices

Fennel fronds for garnish, optional

Place the chicken stock in a medium small saucepan over medium heat. Add the garlic, bay leaf, coriander and fennel seeds and bring to a simmer. Cover and simmer for 10 minutes or until the stock is well flavored. Remove from the heat and set aside to cool.

When cool, strain through a fine mesh sieve, reserving the liquid and the garlic. Discard the remaining solids.

Combine the garlic with the anchovies in a small bowl. Add the oil and, using a kitchen fork, mash the mixture together until quite smooth. Stir in the parsley, capers, orange zest, and vinegar. Season with pepper and set aside.

Place the reserved seasoned chicken stock in a large, shallow saucepan or deep frying pan over medium heat. Add the celery and fennel, cover, and bring to a simmer. Simmer, covered, for about 4 minutes or until barely tender.

Remove from the heat and drain well. Transfer to a warm serving bowl, add the reserved anchovy sauce, season with pepper, and toss to coat. Cover and let marinate for 1 minute.

Uncover and serve, garnished with fennel fronds, if desired.

Nutritional Analysis per Serving: calories 85, carbohydrates 11 g, fiber 5 g, protein 3 g, fat 4 g, sodium 349 mg, sugar 1 g.

KOHLRABI GRATIN

Serves 6

Kohlrabi is quite an underused vegetable, probably because it looks weird and few cooks know what to do with it. In South Asia, it is as popular as carrots are in the United States. Kohlrabi must be thoroughly peeled before being cooked; first off is the outer layer of skin and then a second fibrous layer has to go. So when buying kohlrabi purchase more than you think you need because you are going to lose much of it as you peel. This is another vegetable whose leaves can be eaten, but they are rarely attached unless bought straight from the farm; they might be green or a very beautiful purple-pink.

Butter for greasing casserole
300 ml (½ pint) unsweetened almond milk
2 cloves garlic, halved

2 bay leaves

2 sprigs thyme

½ teaspoon freshly grated nutmeg

1.8 kg (4 lb) kohlrabi, peeled and cut, crosswise, into 3-mm (⅛-inch) thick slices

85 g (3 oz) Parmesan cheese, grated

Salt and white pepper

40 g (1½ oz) unblanched almonds, chopped

Preheat the oven to 200ºC/400ºF/Gas Mark 6.

Generously coat the interior of a 2-liter (3½-pint) casserole or baking dish with butter. Set aside.

Combine the almond milk with the garlic, bay leaves, thyme, and nutmeg in a small saucepan over medium heat. Bring to a simmer; then, immediately remove from the heat.

Place the kohlrabi in a large mixing bowl. Pour the hot milk over the kohlrabi through a fine mesh strainer, discarding the solids. Add two-thirds of the cheese, season with salt and white pepper, and toss to coat.

Using your hands, layer the kohlrabi slices in the casserole, taking care that they are evenly spaced. Pour any remaining milk over the kohlrabi and sprinkle the remaining cheese over the top. Cover with aluminium foil and transfer to the preheated oven. Bake for 30 minutes. Uncover, sprinkle the almonds over the top, and continue to bake for another 15 minutes or until the top is golden brown and the kohlrabi is cooked through.

Remove from the oven and serve.

Nutritional Analysis per Serving: calories 237, carbohydrates 23 g, fiber 5 g, protein 13 g, fat 11 g, sodium 438 mg, sugar 9 g.

CAULIFLOWER WITH LEMON-PARSLEY BUTTER

Serves 4

A wonderfully fragrant sauce accents the sweetness of the roasted cauliflower in this recipe. The nutty crunch of the sunflower seeds adds just that over-the-top extra dimension. This dish can also be served as a warm salad with the addition of chunks of cheese and/or chopped bitter leaves.

1 head white, yellow, purple, or romanesco cauliflower

4 tablespoons ghee

Salt and pepper

Freshly grated zest of 1 lemon

55 g (2 oz) flat-leaf parsley leaves

2 tablespoons lemon juice

2 tablespoons extra virgin olive oil

65 g (2¼ oz) sunflower seeds

Preheat the oven to 220ºC/425ºF/Gas Mark 7.

Cut the cauliflower into florets and place in a mixing bowl. Add the ghee along with salt and pepper to taste and toss to coat. Transfer to a roasting tray and place in the preheated oven. Roast, turning occasionally, for about 25 minutes or until tender and slightly charred.

While the cauliflower is roasting, prepare the sauce.

Place the lemon zest, parsley, lemon juice, and olive oil in the bowl of a food processor fitted with a metal blade and process until almost a purée. Season with salt and pepper to taste.

Remove the cauliflower from the oven and pour the sauce over the top. Add the sunflower seeds and toss to coat.

Serve hot or at room temperature.

Nutritional Analysis per Serving: calories 335, carbohydrates 12 g, fiber 6 g, protein 7 g, fat 31 g, sodium 180 mg, sugar 4 g.

CAULIFLOWER "COUSCOUS"

Serves 4

With so much interest in plant-based diets, cooks have come up with all kinds of inventive methods for cooking vegetables. Turning cauliflower into little couscous-like nuggets is one of the winners. Useful alone when steamed as a base for stews and sauces, it also makes a terrific seasoned side dish. I will give you a couple of ideas of things to do with this vegetable couscous, but I urge you to use your imagination to take it all over the world with the addition of other vegetables, spices, sauces, and/or herbs.

1 head cauliflower (see Note)

Cut the cauliflower into pieces and place them in the bowl of a food processor fitted with the metal blade. Process using quick on and off turns until the cauliflower looks like tiny little nuggets. Watch carefully as it doesn't take long to turn nuggets into purée.

Here is where the fun begins.

You can line a steamer basket with muslin and place the cauliflower in it. Season with salt, cover, and place over boiling water. Steam for about 4 minutes or just until the cauliflower is barely cooked. Again, don't turn it into mush. This gives you a plain couscous-like base for sauces or stews.

Or, you can heat about 2 tablespoons of olive oil in a large frying pan. Add 1 finely diced onion and 1 teaspoon finely chopped garlic and cook, stirring, for about 3 minutes or just until soft. Add the raw cauliflower nuggets, season with salt and pepper to taste, and cook, stirring, for about 5 minutes or until the cauliflower begins to color. Remove from the heat and stir in 1 tablespoon finely chopped fresh herbs of choice, chopped spring onions, chopped olives or sun-dried tomatoes, orange zest, or pomegranate seeds and serve as a side dish. Or, when sautéing the onion and garlic, you can add chopped nuts or pine nuts, diced celery, a couple of handfuls of chopped bitter leaves, or anything you like that might work with the protein or stew you are serving it with.

NOTE Many people discard the core of the cauliflower and use only the florets. I have found that there is absolutely no sound reason for doing this – the core tastes just a bit stronger than the florets and adds at least one more serving to the mix. If you don't have a food processor, you can either grate the cauliflower on the large holes of a box grater or chop it using a very sharp chef's knife.

Nutritional Analysis per Serving (250 ml/8 fl oz): calories 38, carbohydrates 7 g, fiber 4 g, protein 3 g, fat 1 g, sodium 170 mg, sugar 3 g.

SESAME-SCENTED GREEN AND YELLOW BEANS

Serves 4

The mix of green and yellow accented with the black sesame seeds creates a beautiful side dish for almost any protein. If you can't find black sesame seeds, toast some white ones to a nice golden brown.

225 g (8 oz) green beans, trimmed

225 g (8 oz) yellow wax beans, trimmed

1 tablespoon sesame oil

10 g (¼ oz) butter, melted

1 tablespoon black sesame seeds

Salt and pepper

Place the beans in a steamer basket over boiling water. Cover and steam for about 5 minutes or until crisp-tender.

Remove from the steamer and pat dry. Place on a serving plate, add the sesame oil, butter, and sesame seeds, tossing to coat well. Season with salt and pepper to taste and serve hot or at room temperature.

Nutritional Analysis per Serving: calories 91, carbohydrates 7 g, fiber 3 g, protein 2 g, fat 7 g, sodium 152 mg, sugar 3 g.

GREEN BEANS WITH WALNUTS

Serves 4

These beans are a perfect match with almost any meat or fish. The walnuts add an unusual dimension so that everyday green beans become the star of the plate.

    450 g (1 lb) green beans, trimmed and cut, crosswise, into 5-cm
        (2-inch) pieces
    40 g (1½ oz) butter
    50 g (1¾ oz) raw walnuts, chopped
    1 teaspoon freshly grated orange zest
    Salt and pepper

Place the beans in cold, salted water to cover over high heat. Bring to a boil and immediately lower the heat to a simmer. Simmer for about 4 minutes or until crisp-tender.

Remove from the heat and drain well. Pat dry.

Heat the butter in a medium frying pan over medium heat. Add the walnuts and cook, stirring constantly, for about 2 minutes or just until the nuts begin to color. Add the beans and, using tongs, toss and turn to coat well. Season with orange zest, salt, and pepper.

Remove from the pan and serve.

Nutritional Analysis per Serving: calories 171, carbohydrates 8 g, fiber 4 g, protein 4 g, fat 15 g, sodium 151 mg, sugar 3 g.

MEAT

Roast Fillet of Beef Wrapped in Bacon

Steak Diane

Fillet Steak with Compound Butter

London Broil with Grilled Mushrooms

Grilled Spiced Skirt Steak

Southwest-Style Ribeye Steaks

Braised Beef Brisket

Meatloaf Stuffed with Hard-Boiled Eggs

Traditional Chophouse Mixed Grill

Tex-Mex Cowboy Beef Burgers with Tomato-Onion Salsa

Grilled Veal Chops with Rocket

Veal Saltimbocca

Calves Liver and Onions

Roasted Leg of Lamb with Ginger Sauce

Barbecued Butterflied Leg of Lamb with Aubergine
Compote

Lamb and Fennel with Mint Salad

Braised Lamb Shanks with Green Olives

Quick "Moussaka"

Stuffed Pork Loin

Pork Fillet with Sweet Spice Onion Jam

Grilled Pork Chops with Salsa Verde

Gruyère-Glazed Pork Chops

Adobo Pork

Stir-Fried Pork with Watercress

Slow-Roasted Spareribs

ROAST FILLET OF BEEF WRAPPED IN BACON

Serves 6

This is the ultimate dinner party or buffet dish. It can be served hot or at room temperature, and the smoky, fatty bacon is the perfect foil for the tender, mildly flavored meat. A lovely platter of mixed roasted vegetables (see page 106) would make the meal complete and they, too, can be served hot or at room temperature.

675 g (1 lb 8 oz) beef fillet, trimmed of all fat and silverskin
Cracked black pepper
450 g (1 lb) thick-sliced bacon

Preheat the oven to 230ºC/450ºF/Gas Mark 8.

Season the beef with cracked black pepper.

Place the bacon slices, slightly overlapping, on a clean work surface. When finished you should have a rectangle shape large enough to cover the beef. Lay the meat in the center of the bacon rectangle and then pull the bacon up on both sides to completely cover the meat. Using kitchen string, tie the bacon in place around the meat by wrapping the string around the meat in sections about 5 cm (2 inches) apart.

Place the bacon-wrapped beef in the center of a small roasting pan in the preheated oven. Roast for about 25 minutes or until an instant-read thermometer inserted into the center reads 52ºC/125ºF for rare or 60ºC/140ºF for medium-rare.

Remove from the oven and allow to rest for 10 minutes. Cut the string and discard it. Then cut the bacon-wrapped meat, crosswise, into 1-cm (½-inch) thick slices.

Nutritional Analysis per Serving: calories 280, carbohydrates 0 g, fiber 0 g, protein 31 g, fat 15 g, sodium 695 mg, sugar 0 g.

STEAK DIANE

Serves 4

This classic, old-time restaurant dish is easily made at home. The most important thing to remember is that the steaks cook very quickly, and since they are low in fat, if you overcook them they will be dry and tough.

4 x 175-g (6-oz) fillet steaks

Salt and pepper

55 g (2 oz) butter

2 tablespoons extra virgin olive oil

3 tablespoons finely chopped shallots

1 tablespoon cognac

4 tablespoons chopped flat-leaf parsley

2 teaspoons beef stock (low-sodium if desired)

1 teaspoon Dijon mustard

½ teaspoon Worcestershire sauce

Place the steaks on a clean, flat work surface and, using a meat mallet, pound until approximately 1 cm (½ inch) thick.

Season with salt and pepper to taste.

Heat half the butter with the olive oil in a large frying pan over medium-high heat. When very hot but not smoking, add the steaks. Fry for about 90 seconds and turn and fry for another 30 seconds. Do not overcook. Remove the pan from the heat and transfer the steaks to a warm serving platter.

Add the shallots to the pan and return it to medium heat. Stir to blend the shallots into the pan juices and then add the cognac, swirling the pan to combine. Stir in 3 tablespoons of the parsley along with the stock, mustard, and Worcestershire sauce. When blended, stir in the remaining butter. When the butter has melted into the pan sauce, taste and, if necessary, season with salt and pepper to taste.

Pour the sauce over the steaks, sprinkle with the remaining parsley, and serve immediately.

Nutritional Analysis per Serving: calories 425, carbohydrates 2 g, fiber 0 g, protein 33 g, fat 31 g, sodium 401 mg, sugar 1 g.

FILLET STEAK WITH COMPOUND BUTTER

Serves 4

Although fillet steak is extremely tender, because it is low in fat it is not as richly flavored as many other steaks. The melting butter adds just the extra ounce of fat and flavor needed to heighten the beefiness of the steak. Compound butters are easy to make and a boon to keep on hand as they add elegant flavor to all types of grilled meats, poultry, and even fish. The following recipe should yield enough to season quite a few dishes.

4 x 140-g (5-oz) fillet steaks

1 tablespoon extra virgin olive oil

Salt and pepper

4 tablespoons Compound Butter (recipe follows)

Rub the steaks on all sides with the oil and then season with salt and pepper.

Place a heavy-bottom frying pan over high heat. When very hot, add the seasoned steaks and fry, turning occasionally, for about 9 minutes for rare or until they reach the desired degree of doneness on an instant-read thermometer.

Remove from the pan and allow to rest for 2 minutes.

Place 1 tablespoon of Compound Butter on the top of each hot steak, allowing it to melt slightly before serving.

Nutritional Analysis per Serving: calories 346, carbohydrates 1 g, fiber 0 g, protein 27 g, fat 25 g, sodium 285 mg, sugar 0 g.

COMPOUND BUTTER

Makes 225 g (8 oz)

225 g (8 oz) unsalted butter, at room temperature

1 shallot, peeled and finely chopped

1 tablespoon chopped flat-leaf parsley

1 teaspoon lemon juice

Salt and pepper

Combine the butter, shallot, parsley, and lemon juice in the bowl of a food processor fitted with the metal blade and process to thoroughly blend.

Using a rubber spatula, scrape the butter into the center of a piece of clingfilm (or greaseproof paper). Fold the wrap over the butter and, using your hands, form the butter into a neat log shape about 4 cm (1½ inches) in diameter. Tightly close the ends of the plastic wrap and transfer the log to the refrigerator. Chill for at least 1 hour or until firm or freeze for up to 3 months.

When ready to use, unwrap the log and cut the butter, crosswise, into 5-mm (¼-inch) thick slices. Bring to room temperature before serving.

NOTE Other herbs may replace or be combined with the parsley. Tarragon, marjoram, and basil are particularly good ones.

Nutritional Analysis per Serving: calories 102, carbohydrates 1 g, fiber 0 g, protein 0 g, fat 11 g, sodium 37 mg, sugar 0 g.

LONDON BROIL WITH GRILLED MUSHROOMS

Serves 4

This recipe can be made with almost any steak or chop except fillet steak, which is too tender to take a long marination. The steak/

mushroom combination also makes a fantastic salad either on top of or tossed among spicy leaves, such as rocket, and tomatoes or, in fact, almost any other vegetable you like.

An outdoor grill adds lovely flavor to this, but if you don't have one, a stove-top griddle pan is the next best alternative. They are inexpensive and easy to use with the result resembling char-grilled meat.

1 x 565 g (1 lb 4 oz) 4-cm (1½-inch) thick round steak

175 ml (6 fl oz) extra virgin olive oil

4 tablespoons balsamic vinegar

1 teaspoon freshly grated orange zest

4 tablespoons chopped flat-leaf parsley

Salt and pepper

4 large portobello mushroom caps

Place the steak in a large resealable plastic bag along with the oil, vinegar, orange zest, and 1 tablespoon of the parsley. Seal and push the steak around to coat well. Refrigerate for at least 1 hour, but no more than 3 hours.

When ready to grill, remove the meat from the refrigerator and bring to room temperature.

Preheat and oil the grill or alternatively preheat a ridged griddle pan over medium-high heat.

Remove the steak from the plastic bag and season with salt and pepper to taste.

Place the mushroom caps in the plastic bag, seal, and push them around to coat. Season with salt and pepper to taste.

Place the steak along with the mushrooms, top down, on the preheated grill (or in the preheated griddle pan) and grill for 10 minutes.

Turn the steak and grill for another 10 minutes for medium-rare or until it reaches the desired degree of doneness on an instant-read thermometer.

Turn the mushrooms and move them to the outer edge of the grill and grill for another 8 minutes or until just beginning to char. Remove from the grill.

Remove the steak from the grill and set aside for 5 minutes.

Cut the steak and mushrooms into strips and place on a platter. Sprinkle with the remaining parsley and serve.

Nutritional Analysis per Serving: calories 345, carbohydrates 6 g, fiber 2 g, protein 33 g, fat 21 g, sodium 345 mg, sugar 4 g.

GRILLED SPICED SKIRT STEAK
Serves 6

You can make this as hot and spicy as you wish. Mixed peppercorns, available at most supermarkets, are somewhat milder than straight black peppercorns. This sliced steak is terrific as a salad topper or served with an assortment of grilled vegetables (see page 106).

2 tablespoons mixed or black cracked peppercorns

½ teaspoon cayenne pepper or to taste

½ teaspoon hot paprika

½ teaspoon garlic salt

Salt

900-g (2-lb) piece of beef or veal skirt steak

Preheat and oil the grill or alternatively preheat a ridged griddle pan over medium-high heat.

Combine the cracked pepper with the cayenne, paprika, garlic salt, and salt in a small bowl.

Generously coat both sides of the steak with the pepper mix.

Place on the preheated grill (or griddle pan) and grill for 6 minutes. Then, turn and grill for an additional 7 minutes or until medium-rare, or until it reaches the desired degree of doneness on an instant-read thermometer.

Remove the steak from the grill and place on a cutting board to rest for 3 minutes. Cut, on the bias, into thin slices and serve.

Nutritional Analysis per Serving: calories 234, carbohydrates 2 g, fiber 1 g, protein 31 g, fat 11 g, sodium 189 mg, sugar 0 g.

SOUTHWEST-STYLE RIBEYE STEAKS

Serves 4

Ribeye steaks can either be boneless or bone-on; I prefer the latter. A first-class ribeye is well marbled with fat and quite tender. Although grass-fed beef is more readily available, a buffalo ribeye is equally delicious if you can find it. The green chilli sauce is mild and can be used on any meat or poultry to add a hint of zestiness. It keeps, tightly covered and refrigerated, for up to 2 weeks.

450 g (1 lb) fresh mild green chillies

2 tablespoons groundnut oil

225 g (8 oz) onions, peeled and chopped

1 teaspoon finely chopped garlic

250 ml (8 fl oz) beef stock (low-sodium if desired)

Salt and pepper

4 x 340-g (12-oz) 4-cm (1½-inch) thick ribeye steaks

2 tablespoons chilli powder

Preheat the oven to 230ºC/450ºF/Gas Mark 8.

Place the chillies on a nonstick baking tray in the oven and roast for 20 minutes or until well charred. Remove from the oven and allow to cool.

When the chillies are cool enough to handle, peel, stem, and seed.

Heat the oil in a medium saucepan over medium heat. Add the onions and garlic and sauté for 3 minutes. Add the reserved chillies along with the beef stock and salt and pepper to taste. Bring to a simmer and simmer for about 20 minutes or until quite thick.

Remove from the heat and transfer to a blender. Holding down the top with a kitchen towel (to keep the heat from pushing the top off), process until smooth. Transfer to a serving bowl to pass when you serve the steaks.

Preheat and oil the grill or alternatively preheat a ridged griddle pan or cast iron frying pan over medium-high heat.

Season both sides of the steaks with the chilli powder and salt and pepper to taste. Place on the grill (or pan) and grill for 10 minutes. Turn the steak and grill for 12 additional minutes for medium-rare or until cooked to the desired degree of doneness.

Remove from the grill and serve with the sauce on the side.

Nutritional Analysis per Serving: calories 754, carbohydrates 14 g, fiber 3 g, protein 79 g, fat 42 g, sodium 396 mg, sugar 7 g.

BRAISED BEEF BRISKET

Serves 6

You cannot imagine a more flavorful "pot roast" than this brisket. The onions seep into the meat during the slow braise and melt into the most delicious gravy you can imagine.

1.1 kg (2 lb 8 oz) beef brisket

Salt and pepper

2 tablespoons avocado oil

6 large onions, peeled and cut, crosswise, into thin slices

1 tablespoon finely chopped garlic

Season the meat with salt and pepper.

Heat the oil in a cast iron casserole over medium heat. Add the seasoned meat and sear, turning frequently, for about 5 minutes or until nicely browned.

Transfer the meat to a plate. Lay the onions and garlic in the bottom of the pan. Place the meat on top of the onions, cover, and cook for about 2 hours or until the meat is fork tender and the onions have melted into a gravy. After about 1 hour, you can lower the heat, but keep the pan covered or the liquid from the onions will evaporate.

Using tongs, transfer the meat to a cutting board. Using a sharp knife, cut the meat into thin slices. Place on a serving platter and spoon the onion gravy over the top.

Serve immediately.

Nutritional Analysis per Serving: calories 303, carbohydrates 15 g, fiber 3 g, protein 34 g, fat 11 g, sodium 445 mg, sugar 6 g.

MEATLOAF STUFFED WITH HARD-BOILED EGGS

Serves 6

I do wonder what prompted the first cook to place hard-boiled eggs down the center of a meatloaf, but perhaps those many years ago she was already aware of the *Grain Brain* regimen. I say "she" because I am pretty sure it was a home cook and mom in the 1930s who came up with a version of this recipe to feed her hungry family.

340 g (12 oz) minced beef

340 g (12 oz) minced pork

225 g (8 oz) onion, peeled and finely chopped

115 g (4 oz) Parmesan cheese, grated

1 teaspoon finely chopped garlic

1 tablespoon finely chopped basil

1 teaspoon finely chopped oregano

1 large egg, beaten

Salt and pepper

3 large hard-boiled eggs, peeled

125 ml (4 fl oz) beef stock (low-sodium if desired)

100 g (3½ oz) tomatoes, diced, with their juice

1 tablespoon extra virgin olive oil

Preheat the oven to 190ºC/375ºF/Gas Mark 5.

Combine the beef and pork with the onion, grated cheese, garlic, basil, and oregano, using your hands to mix. Add the beaten egg, season with salt and pepper to taste, and continue to mix with your hands until completely blended.

Place half of the meat mixture in a baking dish, forming it into a neat rectangle approximately 10 cm (4 inches) wide in the center of the baking dish. Arrange the hard-boiled eggs down the center of the rectangle. Place the remaining meat over the top of the eggs and, using your hands, enclose the eggs as you form the meat into a neat seamless rectangle.

Combine the beef stock and tomatoes in a small mixing bowl. Season with salt and pepper to taste.

Using a pastry brush, generously coat the exterior of the meatloaf with oil. Pour the beef stock mixture into the dish and transfer to the preheated oven.

Bake, occasionally basting with the pan liquid, for about 45 minutes or until an instant-read thermometer inserted into the thickest part registers 68ºC/155ºF.

Remove from the oven and let rest for about 10 minutes before cutting crosswise into thick slices. Place on a serving platter and spoon any remaining pan juices over the meat. Serve hot or at room temperature.

Nutritional Analysis per Serving: calories 376, carbohydrates 4 g, fiber 1 g, protein 34 g, fat 23 g, sodium 633 mg, sugar 2 g.

TRADITIONAL CHOPHOUSE MIXED GRILL

Serves 4

A mixed grill has been a traditional lunch in men's clubs for generations but is rarely found on menus today. It can have kidneys and sausages added to the mix as well as the meats I use in this recipe. It is often served with a bowl of grainy mustard and some sour pickles. If you don't have an outdoor grill, an oven grill or stove-top griddle pan can be used, but you will most likely have to cook the various ingredients in batches.

2 tomatoes, cored and cut in half, crosswise

Approximately 85 g (3 oz) ghee or unsalted butter, melted

Salt and pepper

2 tablespoons grated Parmesan cheese

2 red onions, peeled and cut in half, crosswise

4 large button mushroom caps

450-g (1-lb) piece of sirloin steak

2 small slices (about 140 g/5 oz total) calves liver

4 small (about 85 g/3 oz) lamb cutlets

4 thick slices (about 85 g/3 oz) bacon or pork belly

Using a pastry brush, lightly coat the top of each tomato half with ghee. Season with salt and pepper to taste and sprinkle with the grated cheese. Set aside.

Run a metal skewer through each onion half to help it hold its shape when grilling. Using a pastry brush, lightly coat the top of each half with ghee and season with salt and pepper to taste. Set aside.

Using a pastry brush, lightly coat the mushrooms with ghee and season with salt and pepper to taste. Set aside.

Preheat and oil the grill or grill pan.

Rub the steak, liver, and lamb cutlets with ghee and season with salt and pepper to taste.

Place the steak in the center of the grill, cover, and grill for 10 minutes. Uncover, turn the steak, and place the liver, lamb cutlets, bacon, tomatoes, onions, and mushrooms on the grill, with the lamb nearest the hotter center. Cover and grill, turning the liver, lamb, bacon, and onion once, for another 10 minutes, for the steak to reach medium-rare and the lamb medium or until it reaches the desired degree of doneness on an instant-read thermometer. At about 6 minutes begin checking the liver, bacon, and vegetables as you don't want them to overcook. If using an oven grill, this will probably have to be done in batches.

Remove all of the meats and vegetables from the grill. Remove the skewer from each onion.

Cut the steak into slices and place an equal portion on each of 4 dinner plates. Place a lamb cutlet, a slice each of liver and bacon along with an onion half, a tomato half, and a mushroom on each plate and serve.

Nutritional Analysis per Serving: calories 502, carbohydrates 11 g, fiber 2 g, protein 41 g, fat 32 g, sodium 480 mg, sugar 5 g.

TEX-MEX COWBOY BEEF BURGERS WITH TOMATO-ONION SALSA

Serves 4

A little Tex-Mex twist to the classic burger that elevates it up and away from the bun and fries. You can make both the burgers and the salsa as hot or as mild as you wish by adjusting the amount of fresh chillies you add.

225 g (8 oz) minced sirloin steak

225 g (8 oz) minced pork

3 tablespoons finely chopped red pepper

2 tablespoons finely chopped red onion

2 teaspoons chilli powder

$1/2$ teaspoon ground cumin

Salt and pepper

4 tablespoons Tomato-Onion Salsa (recipe follows)

Preheat the grill and oil the grill pan or alternatively preheat a stove-top ridged griddle pan or a cast iron frying pan over medium-high heat.

Combine the minced steak and pork with the pepper, onion, chilli powder, cumin, and salt and pepper to taste. Using your hands, mix well to blend. Form the mix into 4 flattened patties of equal size.

Place the patties under the grill (or in the preheated griddle pan or cast iron frying pan) and grill for 5 minutes. Turn and grill for another 5 minutes for medium-well (70ºC/160ºF is sufficient for the beef/pork mix) or until cooked to the desired degree of doneness.

Serve topped with salsa.

Nutritional Analysis per Serving: calories 225, carbohydrates 8 g, fiber 2 g, protein 22 g, fat 12 g, sodium 301 mg, sugar 4 g.

TOMATO-ONION SALSA

Makes about 300 ml (½ pint)

225 g (8 oz) plum tomatoes, peeled, seeded, and coarsely chopped

1 small red onion, peeled and coarsely chopped

1 clove garlic, peeled and finely chopped

$1/2$ teaspoon finely chopped red hot chilli pepper or to taste

$1/2$ teaspoon lime juice

4 tablespoons chopped coriander

Salt and pepper

Combine the tomatoes and onion in a mixing bowl. Stir in the garlic and chilli. When well combined, add the lime juice. Fold in the coriander and season with salt and pepper to taste. If not serving immediately, cover and refrigerate for no more than 8 hours.

Nutritional Analysis per Serving (4 tablespoons): calories 22, carbohydrates 5 g, fiber 1 g, protein 1 g, fat 0 g, sodium 77 mg, sugar 3 g.

GRILLED VEAL CHOPS WITH ROCKET

Serves 4

If you don't have a stove-top ridged griddle pan, please get one. Of course, they don't impart the scent of burning wood or charcoal to the meat, but they mark the meat beautifully and make it possible to grill all year round. And, this is a recipe that you will want to make every month of the year. It works well with pork chops, too.

2 tablespoons extra virgin olive oil

1 tablespoon lemon juice

4 x 200-g (7-oz) veal chops

Salt and pepper

325 g (11½ oz) well-washed rocket leaves

75 ml (3 fl oz) Balsamic Vinaigrette (see page 35)

Preheat the grill and oil the grill pan or preheat a ridged griddle pan over medium-high heat.

Combine the olive oil and lemon juice and generously coat the chops with it. Season with salt and pepper to taste.

Place the chops under the grill (or in the griddle pan) and grill, turning occasionally, for about 10 minutes or until an instant-read thermometer registers 55ºC/130ºF for medium.

Remove from the grill and let rest for 5 minutes.

Place the rocket in a mixing bowl and drizzle about half of the vinaigrette over the leaves, tossing to coat.

Place an equal portion of the dressed rocket in the center of each of 4 dinner plates. Place a chop on top, drizzle with the remaining vinaigrette, and serve.

Nutritional Analysis per Serving: calories 354, carbohydrates 2 g, fiber 0 g, protein 25 g, fat 28 g, sodium 455 mg, sugar 1 g.

VEAL SALTIMBOCCA

Serves 4

This classic Mediterranean dish is popular in Italy, Spain, and parts of Greece. In Rome, the sauce is usually made with Marsala wine, which has some sweetness. You can also add capers to the finishing sauce for a hint of saltiness.

2 tablespoons plus 1 teaspoon chopped sage

2 tablespoons chopped rosemary

2 teaspoons finely chopped garlic

4 veal escalopes

4 slices Parma ham

155 g (5½ oz) butter

2 tablespoons extra virgin olive oil

Salt and pepper

125 ml (4 fl oz) dry white wine

2 tablespoons lemon juice

Combine 2 tablespoons of the sage with the rosemary and garlic in a small mixing bowl.

Place the veal escalopes on a clean, flat work surface. Working with one piece at a time, evenly cover each piece with the herb mixture. Then, cover the herb layer with a slice of Parma ham.

Starting at one end, firmly roll the veal escalopes into a cigar-like shape. Using kitchen string, tie each veal parcel together by tying one loop of string around the center and another loop around the length of the parcel.

Place 115 g (4 oz) of the butter and the olive oil in a large frying pan over medium heat. When melted, season the veal parcels with salt and pepper to taste and place them into the hot pan. Cook, turning occasionally, for about 5 minutes or until nicely colored on all sides. Add the wine and lemon juice and bring to a simmer. Lower the heat, cover, and cook at a bare simmer for 20 minutes or until cooked through.

Using tongs, place the veal parcels on a serving platter. Using kitchen scissors, carefully cut the ties.

Raise the heat to high under the frying pan and whisk in the remaining 40 g (1½ oz) butter and 1 teaspoon sage. Taste and, if necessary, season with salt and pepper to taste. Pour over the veal and serve immediately.

Nutritional Analysis per Serving: calories 644, carbohydrates 3 g, fiber 0 g, protein 32 g, fat 53 g, sodium 625 mg, sugar 0 g.

CALVES LIVER AND ONIONS

Serves 4

Liver is one of those meats that people either love or hate. It is often overcooked, tough, and dry, but if you cook it carefully and quickly, liver is tender and mildly flavored. With the accent of sweet red onions it becomes a "can I have seconds" kind of dish.

85 g (3 oz) butter

3 tablespoons extra virgin olive oil plus more for brushing the pan

5 large red onions, peeled and cut, crosswise, into thin slices

Salt and pepper

3 tablespoons balsamic vinegar

450 g (1 lb) calves liver, cut into thick slices

Combine two-thirds of the butter with 1 tablespoon of the olive oil in a large frying pan over medium heat. When melted, add the onions and season with salt and pepper to taste. Lower the heat and cook, stirring occasionally, for 20 minutes or until the onions have exuded most of their liquid. Add the vinegar and continue to cook for an additional 10 minutes. Stir in the remaining butter and when melted, remove the onions from the heat, but keep them warm.

Using the remaining 2 tablespoons of olive oil, generously coat each slice of liver. Season with salt and pepper to taste.

Preheat a ridged griddle pan over medium-high heat. When hot, brush with additional olive oil. Add the seasoned liver and cook, turning once, for about 4 minutes or until nicely browned on each side. Do not overcook as the liver will quickly toughen.

Remove from the heat and place the liver on a serving platter. Top with the warm onions and serve.

Nutritional Analysis per Serving: calories 459, carbohydrates 22 g, fiber 3 g, protein 23 g, fat 32 g, sodium 648 mg, sugar 9 g.

ROASTED LEG OF LAMB WITH GINGER SAUCE

Serves 6

Generally a leg of lamb is butterflied for grilling, and if you cook a small one, the whole leg can be grilled. I prefer roasting in a very hot oven for the first 15 minutes; then, I turn the temperature down to finish cooking. This recipe can be used for larger legs of lamb; roasting requires about 22 minutes per 450 g (1 lb) for rare or until a meat thermometer registers the degree of doneness you desire.

If you don't want to make the Ginger Sauce, mix some fresh herbs (any combination you like) with the olive oil and rub into the meat instead. The herbs alone will add a hint of freshness to the juicy, deeply flavored lamb.

Small leg of lamb (about 1.6 kg/3 lb 8 oz), trimmed of excess fat

4 tablespoons extra virgin olive oil

Salt and pepper

225 g (8 oz) tomatoes, peeled, seeded, and coarsely chopped

1 tablespoon grated ginger root

1 teaspoon chopped garlic

4 tablespoons dry white wine

25 g (1 oz) butter, at room temperature

4 tablespoons chopped mint leaves

Preheat the oven to 230ºC/450ºF/Gas Mark 8.

Generously coat the lamb with the oil and season with salt and pepper to taste. Place on a rack in a small roasting pan and roast, turning occasionally, for about 15 minutes or until nicely browned on all sides. Reduce the oven temperature to 160ºC/325ºF/Gas Mark 3 and continue to roast, without turning, for about 50 minutes or until a meat thermometer registers 60ºC/140ºF for rare or until cooked to the desired degree of doneness (74ºC/165ºF will give you very well-done meat).

While the meat is roasting, prepare the sauce.

Combine the tomatoes, ginger, and garlic in the bowl of a food processor fitted with a metal blade. Process, using quick on and off turns, to make a chunky mix. Transfer to a small nonreactive saucepan over medium heat and bring to a simmer. Simmer, stirring frequently, for 5 minutes.

Add the wine along with the butter and season with salt and pepper to taste. Return to a simmer and simmer for an additional 5 minutes or just long enough to allow the alcohol to evaporate slightly. Remove from the heat and fold in the mint. Keep warm until ready to serve.

Remove the lamb from the oven and set aside to rest for a couple of minutes.

Using a sharp knife, slice the meat across the grain and place on a platter. Serve with the warm sauce on the side.

Nutritional Analysis per Serving: calories 371, carbohydrates 2 g, fiber 0 g, protein 36 g, fat 23 g, sodium 282 mg, sugar 1 g.

BARBECUED BUTTERFLIED LEG OF LAMB WITH AUBERGINE COMPOTE

Serves 6

Lamb and aubergine are two well-known partners in Greek cooking, and this recipe is an undemanding one that seals the marriage. Grilling makes it a warm weather dish, but the lamb can also be roasted (see page 153) so quickly and effortlessly it becomes a dish to be made year-round. Both the meat and the compote can be served at room temperature.

175 ml (6 fl oz) extra virgin olive oil

1 tablespoon lemon juice

1 tablespoon celery seeds

1 teaspoon ground cumin

1 teaspoon smoked paprika

1.4 kg (3 lb) butterflied leg of lamb (see Note)

1 medium aubergine, trimmed and cut, crosswise, into 1-cm
    (1/2-inch) thick slices

2 large tomatoes, cut in half, crosswise

Salt and pepper

115 g (4 oz) onion, peeled and finely chopped

4 tablespoons coarsely chopped green Greek olives

1 tablespoon roasted garlic

1 tablespoon red wine vinegar

2 teaspoons chopped capers

1 tablespoon chopped flat-leaf parsley

Combine 125 ml (4 fl oz) of the olive oil with the lemon juice, celery seeds, cumin, and paprika. Generously coat the lamb with the oil mixture, reserving any remaining for later use. Set the lamb aside to marinate for 30 minutes.

Preheat and oil the barbecue. Alternatively, preheat the oven to 200°C/400°F/Gas Mark 6.

Using the remaining 50 ml (2 fl oz) of the olive oil, generously coat the aubergine and tomatoes. Season with salt and pepper to taste.

Place the vegetables on the preheated barbecue and grill the aubergine, turning occasionally, for about 8 minutes or until nicely charred and just cooked through.

Grill the tomatoes, skin side down, without turning, for about 4 minutes or just until slightly soft. Remove the vegetables from the grill and set aside.

Alternatively place the aubergine and tomatoes on a roasting tray in the preheated oven and roast, turning occasionally, for about 15 minutes for the aubergine and 10 minutes for the tomatoes. If you are also roasting the lamb, do not turn off the oven.

Season the lamb with salt and pepper to taste and place on the hot grill. Grill, turning occasionally and brushing with the reserved oil mixture, for 12 minutes. Move the lamb to the cooler part of the grill. Cover and continue to grill, turning and brushing with the oil mixture from time to time, for about 18 minutes or until an instant-read thermometer inserted into the thickest part reads 60°C/140°F for rare or until cooked to the desired degree of doneness. Alternatively place the lamb on a rack in a roasting pan in the preheated oven and roast for about 30 minutes or until it reaches the same degree of doneness as for grilling.

While the meat is grilling, make the compote.

Place the aubergine and tomatoes in the bowl of a food processor fitted with a metal blade. Process, using quick on and off turns, until just barely chopped.

Transfer to a mixing bowl and stir in the onion, olives, garlic, vinegar, and capers. Season with salt and pepper to taste and set aside for 30 minutes to allow the flavors to blend. Fold in the parsley and transfer to a serving bowl.

Remove the lamb from the barbecue or oven and set aside to rest for a couple of minutes.

Using a sharp knife, slice the meat across the grain and place on a platter. Serve with the compote on the side.

NOTE A butterflied leg of lamb is simply a leg of lamb from which the bone has been removed and then the meat split down but not through the center to open it up. The meat is then flattened slightly to resemble a butterfly. Most butchers will be happy to do this for you.

Nutritional Analysis per Serving: calories 450, carbohydrates 10 g, fiber 3 g, protein 43 g, fat 27 g, sodium 469 mg, sugar 4 g.

LAMB AND FENNEL WITH MINT SALAD
Serves 4

Here is another lamb recipe that is scented with the flavors of Greece – fennel, feta, olive oil, mint, and oregano (if you can find it, Greek oregano has wonderful qualities of its own). This is a light and beautiful dish that serves well as both a weekday dinner and a company's-coming sensation.

3 large fennel bulbs

4 tablespoons extra virgin olive oil

2 tablespoons red wine vinegar

2 tablespoons chopped oregano

Salt and cracked black pepper

565 g (1 lb 4 oz) boneless lamb loin

75 g (2¾ oz) mint leaves

140 g (5 oz) feta cheese, crumbled

1 tablespoon freshly grated orange zest

1 tablespoon lemon juice

2 tablespoons toasted pumpkin seeds

Preheat the oven to 200ºC/400ºF/Gas Mark 6.

Line a roasting tray with parchment paper and set aside.

Trim off any dark or damaged pieces from the fennel bulbs, leaving the bulb intact and reserving the fronds. Using a sharp knife, cut the fennel bulbs, lengthwise, into slices. You will need 8 slices.

Chop enough of the fronds to yield 1 tablespoon, reserving the remainder in their feathery state for the salad (you will need about 5 tablespoons).

Combine the oil, vinegar, and oregano with the chopped fennel fronds. Season the mix with salt and cracked pepper. Generously coat the fennel slices and the lamb with the oil mixture.

Lay the fennel slices out on the baking sheet and place the lamb on a rack in a small roasting pan. Transfer both to the preheated oven and roast for about 12 minutes or until the fennel is nicely colored and cooked through and the lamb is cooked to 60ºC/140ºF for rare or until cooked to the desired degree of doneness.

While the fennel and lamb are cooking, make the salad.

Combine the mint with the reserved fennel fronds and the feta. Sprinkle the orange zest and lemon juice over the top and season with salt and pepper to taste. Toss to coat.

Using a sharp knife, cut the lamb, crosswise, into thick slices.

Place 2 slices of the roasted fennel in the center of each of 4 dinner plates. Top with an equal portion of the sliced lamb. Mound the salad on top, sprinkle with pumpkin seeds, and serve immediately.

Nutritional Analysis per Serving: calories 565, carbohydrates 11 g, fiber 4 g, protein 34 g, fat 44 g, sodium 720 mg, sugar 5 g.

BRAISED LAMB SHANKS WITH GREEN OLIVES

Serves 4

In recent years, lamb shanks have become the go-to comfort food. They are meaty, flavorful, and manageable to cook as they are usually braised. You can put them together in the morning and go about your day while they simmer away. Then, dinner is on the table in minutes.

3 tablespoons extra virgin olive oil

4 whole lamb shanks

Salt and pepper

225 g (8 oz) leeks, cleaned and chopped, with some green part

1 tablespoon finely chopped garlic

1 rib celery, peeled and chopped

150 g (5¼ oz) swede, peeled and diced

250 ml (8 fl oz) dry red wine

750 ml (1¼ pints) Chicken Stock (see page 33) or low-sodium chicken stock

2 x 400-ml (14-oz) cans chopped tomatoes with their juice

1 teaspoon finely chopped rosemary

1 teaspoon finely chopped thyme

1 teaspoon finely chopped basil

1 teaspoon finely chopped flat-leaf parsley

250 g (9 oz) pitted green olives

Preheat the oven to 180ºC/350ºF/Gas Mark 4.

Heat the oil in a cast iron casserole over medium heat. Season the lamb shanks with salt and pepper to taste and add them to the hot oil. Sear, turning occasionally, until all sides are browned. Using tongs, transfer the browned shanks to a platter.

Remove all but 1 tablespoon of fat from the pan. Add the leeks and garlic and sauté for 3 minutes. Stir in the celery and swede and continue cooking for another 4 minutes.

Add the red wine to the pan, raise the heat, and bring to a boil. Boil, stirring constantly with a wooden spoon to release all of the browned bits in the bottom of the pan, for about 7 minutes or until the wine has begun to evaporate.

Add the chicken stock and again bring to a boil. Stir in the tomatoes, rosemary, thyme, basil, and parsley and once again bring to a boil.

Return the shanks to the pan and season with salt and pepper to taste. Cover, transfer to the preheated oven, and braise for 1 hour. Uncover, add the olives, and continue to braise for another hour or until the meat is almost falling off the bone.

Remove from the oven and serve.

NOTE Lamb shanks may be stored, covered and refrigerated, for up to 3 days or tightly sealed and frozen for up to 3 months.

Nutritional Analysis per Serving: calories 472, carbohydrates 20 g, fiber 3 g, protein 30 g, fat 25 g, sodium 768 mg, sugar 9 g.

QUICK "MOUSSAKA"

Serves 4

Moussaka, a traditional Greek dish, is made with a rich béchamel sauce along with lamb, tomatoes, aubergine, breadcrumbs, and lots of sweet spice. This is a very modest version that takes no time to put together and is just as delicious reheated the next day. If you love cinnamon and allspice, you can add about ½ teaspoon of each to the lamb mixture for a slightly different flavor.

2 tablespoons avocado oil

1 large courgette

450 g (1 lb) minced lamb

1 tablespoon chopped flat-leaf parsley

1 teaspoon chopped oregano plus more for garnish, if desired

1 teaspoon finely chopped garlic

1 large egg

Salt and pepper

140 g (5 oz) crumbled feta cheese

8 aubergine slices, about 8 mm (⅓ inch) thick and 15 cm

    (6 inches) long

240 g (8½ oz) sheep's milk ricotta cheese

100 g (3½ oz) mozzarella cheese, grated

Preheat the oven to 180ºC/350ºF/Gas Mark 4.

Line a 28-cm (11-inch) rectangular baking dish with parchment paper. Using 1 tablespoon of the avocado oil, generously coat the paper. Set aside.

Grate the courgette and place it in clean kitchen paper. Tightly twist the paper together and squeeze out as much of the liquid as you can.

Combine the drained courgette with the lamb, parsley, oregano, and garlic, stirring to blend. Add the egg along with salt and pepper to taste and, using your hands, blend the mixture together. Add the feta and carefully mix – you want to blend, but not completely mash the cheese.

Lay 4 slices of the aubergine out in a single layer in the prepared baking dish. Top each piece with an equal portion of the lamb, patting down to make a smooth, even coating. Top each piece with a slice of aubergine. Using a pastry brush, generously coat the aubergine with the remaining 1 tablespoon avocado oil.

Combine the ricotta and mozzarella. When mixed, place an equal portion on top of the oiled aubergine slices, again smoothing to make an even cover.

Transfer to the preheated oven and bake for about 45 minutes or until the top is golden brown and the lamb is completely cooked.

Remove from the oven and sprinkle with oregano, if desired.

Place an individual "moussaka" on each of 4 dinner plates and serve with a lovely tossed green salad on the side, if desired.

Nutritional Analysis per Serving: calories 657, carbohydrates 22 g, fiber 2 g, protein 48 g, fat 52 g, sodium 780 mg, sugar 6 g.

STUFFED PORK LOIN

Serves 6

Free-range pork has a much richer flavor and deeper texture than commercially raised pork. The walnuts and walnut oil add a unique taste that marries very well with the pork. This recipe is a wonderful Sunday supper or dinner party dish that can be served with more sautéed Swiss chard on the side.

1.4 kg (3 lb) boneless pork loin

40 g (1½ oz) unsalted butter

225 g (8 oz) Swiss chard, chopped

115 g (4 oz) onion, peeled and finely chopped

1 teaspoon finely chopped garlic

Salt and pepper

2 tablespoons walnut oil

250 ml (8 fl oz) white wine

75 g (2¾ oz) raw walnuts, chopped

Preheat the oven to 200ºC/400ºF/Gas Mark 6.

Using a sharp knife, carefully cut the pork open to make a neat, flat solid piece of meat. This is best done by cutting from one side into the center (without cutting through to the edge) and then carefully folding the cut flap out. Then, cut from the interior out through the thicker piece to open another flap. Gently push down to flatten the entire piece out. Cover with clingfilm and let the pork come to room temperature.

Place the butter in a medium frying pan over medium heat. Add the chard, onion, and garlic and sauté for about 4 minutes or until softened. Season with salt and pepper to taste.

Uncover the pork and carefully cover with an even layer of the chard stuffing, leaving about 2.5 cm (1 inch) around the edges. Roll, cigar fashion, from the bottom up to make a neat log. Using kitchen string, tie the roll closed. Rub the exterior with walnut oil and again season with salt and pepper to taste.

Transfer the loin to a roasting pan along with the wine. Place in the preheated oven and roast for 30 minutes or until nicely colored. Add the walnuts, lower the heat to 190ºC/375ºF/Gas Mark 5, and roast for an additional hour or until an instant-read thermometer reads 70ºC/160ºF when inserted into the thickest part.

Remove from the oven and let rest for 15 minutes.

Untie and cut, crosswise, into thin slices. Drizzle the pan juices and sprinkle the walnuts over the sliced meat and serve.

Nutritional Analysis per Serving: calories 407, carbohydrates 4 g, fiber 2 g, protein 46 g, fat 23 g, sodium 356 mg, sugar 1 g.

PORK FILLET WITH SWEET SPICE ONION JAM

Serves 4

A simple dish that is simply delish! Pork fillet cooks quickly and the jam can be made in advance, so this is a quick weekday-night dinner in the making. Be careful when you roast the meat; it will be tough if overcooked.

565 g (1 lb 4 oz) pork fillet
1 tablespoon extra virgin olive oil
Salt and pepper
125 ml (4 fl oz) Sweet Spice Onion Jam (recipe follows)

Preheat the oven to 200ºC/400ºF/Gas Mark 6.

Using your hands, rub the entire fillet with olive oil. Generously season with salt and pepper to taste.

Place the meat in a large, ovenproof frying pan over high heat. Sear, turning frequently, until all sides are browned. Transfer to the preheated oven and roast for about 20 minutes or until an instant-read thermometer reads 63ºC/145ºF.

Remove from the oven and let rest for 5 minutes before cutting, crosswise, into thin slices.

Spread the onion jam on a serving platter and then place the pork in slightly overlapping slices down the center. Serve immediately.

Nutritional Analysis per Serving (includes 2 tablespoons onion jam): calories 221, carbohydrates 4 g, fiber 1 g, protein 27 g, fat 10 g, sodium 241 mg, sugar 2 g.

SWEET SPICE ONION JAM

Makes about 750 ml (1¼ pints)

115 g (4 oz) unsalted butter

2.3 kg (5 lb) red onions, peeled and sliced

3 tablespoons balsamic vinegar

2 teaspoons ground cinnamon

½ teaspoon ground cloves

½ teaspoon ground cardamom

Salt and pepper

Melt the butter in a large sauté pan over medium-low heat. Add the onions, lower the heat, cover, and cook, stirring occasionally, for about 30 minutes or until very soft. Stir in the vinegar, cinnamon, cloves, and cardamom, season with salt and pepper to taste, and continue to cook for another 15 minutes or until the onions are jam-like and almost falling apart.

Remove from the heat and serve or allow to cool and store, covered and refrigerated, for up to 1 week.

Nutritional Analysis per Serving (2 tablespoons): calories 41, carbohydrates 4 g, fiber 1 g, protein 1 g, fat 3 g, sodium 38 mg, sugar 2 g.

GRILLED PORK CHOPS WITH SALSA VERDE

Serves 4

What could be easier than throwing a few chops on the grill? Nothing that I know of, but I do add a little time by brining the meat in a salty-herby mix. This tenderizes the meat and adds some flavor. The salsa keeps well for a few days, covered and refrigerated, and can be used with almost any type of meat or fish.

3 tablespoons salt

4 sprigs flat-leaf parsley

4 sprigs thyme

4 x 140-g (5-oz) thick-cut pork chops

Salt and pepper

125 ml (4 fl oz) Salsa Verde (recipe follows)

Combine the salt, parsley, and thyme in a resealable plastic bag. Add the chops along with enough cold water to completely cover them. Seal the bag and refrigerate for 1 hour.

When ready to cook, preheat the grill and oil the grill pan. Alternatively preheat a stove-top ridged griddle pan over medium-high heat.

Drain the chops and pat them dry. Season with salt and pepper to taste and place under the preheated grill (or in the preheated griddle pan). Grill, turning occasionally to nicely mark the meat, for about 15 minutes or until an instant-read thermometer reads 63ºC/145ºF. A griddle pan will generally cook the chops in about the same time.

Remove from the grill and let rest for 10 minutes to finish cooking. Serve with Salsa Verde on the side.

Nutritional Analysis per Serving (includes 2 tablespoons Salsa Verde): calories 199, carbohydrates 1 g, fiber 0 g, protein 20 g, fat 13 g, sodium 704 mg, sugar 0 g.

SALSA VERDE

Makes about 500 ml (17 fl oz)

½ bunch spinach, well washed and finely chopped, stems included

1 shallot, peeled and finely chopped

2 teaspoons finely chopped spring onion

1 teaspoon freshly grated orange zest

125 ml (4 fl oz) extra virgin olive oil

1 tablespoon red wine vinegar

Salt and pepper

Combine the spinach, shallot, spring onion, and orange zest in a mixing bowl. Add the olive oil and vinegar and season with salt and pepper to taste. Taste and, if necessary, add more vinegar for a zesty salsa. (If you decide to do all of this in a food processor, do not over-process; you want some texture and you don't want to emulsify the oil.)

Nutritional Analysis per Serving (2 tablespoons): calories 64, carbohydrates 1 g, fiber 0 g, protein 0 g, fat 7 g, sodium 81 mg, sugar 0 g.

GRUYÈRE-GLAZED PORK CHOPS

Serves 4

Only the French would make a good thing better by adding cheese to it, because who else would have thought to glaze meat with cheese? The chops must be fully cooked before being glazed. And, the glaze should be golden brown and bubbly as the chops come to the table.

1 egg yolk

115 g (4 oz) Gruyère cheese, grated

1 tablespoon whole grain mustard

1 tablespoon almond milk

1 tablespoon chopped chives

4 loin pork chops, approximately 140 g (5 oz) each

Salt and pepper

1 tablespoon coconut oil

Preheat the grill.

Combine the egg yolk with the cheese, mustard, milk, and chives in a small mixing bowl. Using a wooden spoon, stir and mash until completely soft and blended. Set aside.

Season the chops with salt and pepper.

Heat the oil in a large frying pan over medium-high heat. Add the seasoned chops and fry, turning occasionally, for about 15 minutes or until both sides are nicely browned.

Remove the chops from the frying pan and carefully coat one side of each chop with an equal portion of the cheese mixture.

Place the coated chops on a grill pan under the preheated grill. Grill for about 3 minutes or until the cheese is golden brown, bubbling, and glazed.

Remove from the grill and serve.

Nutritional Analysis per Serving: calories 328, carbohydrates 2 g, fiber 0 g, protein 35 g, fat 20 g, sodium 243 mg, sugar 0 g.

ADOBO PORK

Serves 4

This is based on a traditional pork dish from the Philippines, where both pork and coconut are used in many, many recipes. The heat of the big dose of pepper is tempered by the coconut milk. I like to serve this dish with Fried Green Plantains (see page 125).

1½ tablespoons coconut oil

1 medium onion, peeled and sliced

1 tablespoon finely chopped garlic

450 g (1 lb) pork fillet, cubed

About 1 tablespoon pepper

2 bay leaves

1 tablespoon white vinegar

350 ml (12 fl oz) unsweetened coconut milk

2 tablespoons toasted unsweetened coconut flakes

Heat the oil in a large saucepan over medium heat. Add the onion and garlic and cook, stirring frequently, for about 5 minutes or until beginning to color. Do not allow the garlic to burn. Add the pork, season with the pepper, and cook for another 5 minutes or just until the pork begins to color.

Stir in the bay leaves and vinegar along with 175 ml (6 fl oz) water. Bring to a simmer and simmer for 20 minutes or until the pork is just cooked.

Add the coconut milk and continue to cook for another 10 minutes or until the pork is very tender.

Remove from the heat and serve, sprinkled with toasted coconut.

Nutritional Analysis per Serving: calories 356, carbohydrates 8 g, fiber 1 g, protein 23 g, fat 26 g, sodium 72 mg, sugar 1 g.

STIR-FRIED PORK WITH WATERCRESS

Serves 4

We often think of watercress as that sprig of garnish on a restaurant plate, but it is far more useful than that. It can be sautéed for a side vegetable for almost any meat, but you don't want to overcook it. In this recipe, the hot meat wilts it just enough, leaving a little crunch and lots of spice.

2 tablespoons coconut oil

1 tablespoon finely chopped garlic

1 tablespoon finely chopped ginger root

450 g (1 lb) pork fillet, cut into bite-sized pieces

Salt and pepper

450 g (1 lb) watercress, trimmed of tough stems

65 g (2¼ oz) sunflower seeds

1 teaspoon freshly grated orange zest

Heat the oil in a wok or large frying pan over medium-high heat. Add the garlic and ginger and cook, stirring constantly, for about 2 minutes or until lightly colored. Add the pork and season with salt and pepper to taste. Cook, occasionally tossing and turning, for 5 minutes or until the pork is no longer pink and has begun to color around the edges.

Remove from the heat and toss in the watercress, sunflower seeds, and orange zest. Serve immediately.

Nutritional Analysis per Serving: calories 300, carbohydrates 6 g, fiber 2 g, protein 28 g, fat 19 g, sodium 385 mg, sugar 1 g.

SLOW-ROASTED SPARERIBS

Serves 4

Who thinks of spareribs in the middle of winter? With this recipe you will, although you can also slow-roast these on the barbecue in the summer. You can easily vary the spices for the rub using any that appeal to you, but always add a little heat by including chilli powder or cayenne. The heat sinks into the ribs and turns them into a tantalizing lick-your-fingers dish.

1.8 kg (4 lb) spareribs

1 tablespoon chilli powder

½ tablespoon ground cumin

½ tablespoon black pepper

1 teaspoon salt

1 teaspoon ground cinnamon

1 teaspoon cayenne or to taste

Place the spareribs on a roasting tray.

Combine the chilli powder, cumin, pepper, salt, cinnamon, and cayenne in a small mixing bowl. When blended, using your hands, coat both sides of the ribs with the spice rub. Cover with clingfilm and set aside to marinate for at least 1 hour or refrigerate for up to 8 hours. If refrigerated, bring to room temperature before roasting.

Preheat the oven to 150ºC/300ºF/Gas Mark 2.

Unwrap the ribs and cover with aluminium foil, taking care to seal it all around. Place in the preheated oven and roast for about 2½ hours or until the ribs are completely cooked through and almost falling off the bone.

Remove from the oven and serve, with plenty of napkins.

Nutritional Analysis per Serving: calories 711, carbohydrates 2 g, fiber 1 g, protein 52 g, fat 54 g, sodium 746 mg, sugar 0 g.

POULTRY

Perfect Roast Chicken

Pesto-Roasted Chicken

Barbecued Coconut-Sesame Chicken with Jicama-Cucumber Relish

Chicken with 40 Cloves of Garlic

Chicken Breasts Stuffed with Swiss Chard and Goat Cheese

Jerk Chicken

Baked Chicken Parcels

Chicken Curry with Coriander Chutney

Chicken with Lemon and Olives

Sesame Chicken

Herb-Roasted Turkey Breast

Turkey Steaks with Roasted Peppers and Cheese

Spicy Turkey Meatballs in Tomato Sauce

PERFECT ROAST CHICKEN

Serves 4

You have to think a bit ahead to make this chicken, but it is well worth the time. You will get moist, juicy meat and unbelievably crisp skin. I like to put a couple of lemon halves in the pan for the last 15 minutes and then squirt some hot lemon juice on the meat when I serve it.

1.6 kg (3 lb 8 oz) roasting chicken
Sea salt

Rinse the chicken under cold running water and pat it dry. Generously coat the exterior with sea salt – all of the skin should be covered.

Place the salted chicken in a shallow bowl, cover with clingfilm, and place in the refrigerator for 48 hours.

One hour before ready to roast, preheat the oven to 230ºC/450ºF/Gas Mark 8.

Remove the chicken from the refrigerator and set it aside to come to room temperature.

About 30 minutes before roasting, place a small roasting pan in the oven to heat it up.

Uncover the chicken, push off any remaining salt, and carefully pat the skin dry.

Place a rack in the roasting pan and then place the salted chicken onto the rack. Roast for about 45 minutes or until the chicken is cooked through and the skin is golden brown and very crisp.

Remove from the oven and let rest for 10 minutes before carving.

Nutritional Analysis per Serving: calories 451, carbohydrates 0 g, fiber 0 g, protein 52 g, fat 26 g, sodium 735 mg, sugar 0 g.

PESTO-ROASTED CHICKEN

Serves 4

This is an extraordinarily flavorful roast chicken. It takes a little patience to stuff the seasoned ricotta under the skin, but the end result is well worth the effort. The extra Pesto you'll make keeps well and is terrific on roasted vegetables or as a seasoning for a basic vinaigrette.

1.6 kg (3 lb 8 oz) roasting chicken

480 g (1 lb 1 oz) fresh sheep's milk ricotta

75 ml (⅛ pint) Pesto (recipe follows)

Salt and pepper

150 g (5¼ oz) butter

1 lemon

Preheat the oven to 200ºC/400ºF/Gas Mark 6.

Rinse the chicken under cold running water and pat dry. Place it on a clean cutting board.

Combine the ricotta with the Pesto, beating to blend completely. Taste and, if necessary, season with salt and pepper to taste.

Using your fingertips, carefully push back the skin from both sides of the chicken breast to loosen it from the flesh. Working downward, push your fingertips into the leg to loosen the skin around the thigh and leg on both sides. Then, working with just a small handful of the ricotta mixture at a time, scoop it up and begin patting it over the flesh wherever you have loosened the skin. You should end up with a smooth, even layer of the ricotta over all of the flesh.

Place the butter in a small pan over very low heat and cook just until melted.

Using a zester, remove the zest from the lemon and combine it with the melted butter. Cut the lemon in half, crosswise, and place it in the cavity of the chicken.

Pull the chicken legs up and against the body and tie the ends of the legs together with kitchen string. Lift the wing tips up and tuck them under the chicken.

Using a pastry brush lightly coat the exterior of the chicken with the lemon-butter and season with salt and pepper to taste.

Place the chicken on a rack in a small roasting pan and transfer to the preheated oven. Roast, generously basting frequently with the lemon-scented butter, for about 45 minutes or until the skin is golden brown, the ricotta has puffed somewhat, and a meat thermometer inserted into the thickest part reads 70ºC/160ºF.

Remove the chicken from the oven and let rest for 10 minutes.

Using a sharp knife, cut the chicken into serving pieces and serve immediately.

Nutritional Analysis per Serving: calories 622, carbohydrates 7 g, fiber 0 g, protein 59 g, fat 43 g, sodium 511 mg, sugar 1 g.

PESTO

Makes about 600 ml (1 pint)

150 g (5¼ oz) basil leaves

4 tablespoons toasted pine nuts

1 teaspoon chopped garlic

250 ml (8 fl oz) extra virgin olive oil

55 g (2 oz) Parmesan cheese, grated

Salt and pepper

Combine the basil with the pine nuts and garlic in the bowl of a food processor fitted with a metal blade and process just until chopped. With the motor running, begin slowly adding about half of the olive oil, processing until blended. Don't overprocess as you want to see tiny bits of basil. Scrape the purée from the processor bowl into a small mixing bowl. Stir in the cheese and season with salt and pepper to taste. Begin beating in the remaining olive oil until a thick purée is formed.

If not using immediately, scrape the pesto into a clean, glass container. Smooth the top and then cover it with a thin layer of olive oil; this will keep the pesto from discoloring. Refrigerate until ready to use or up to 2 weeks. Or, alternatively, freeze for up to 3 months, and then thaw before using.

Nutritional Analysis per Serving: calories 123, carbohydrates 0 g, fiber 0 g, protein 2 g, fat 13 g, sodium 63 mg, sugar 0 g.

BARBECUED COCONUT-SESAME CHICKEN WITH JICAMA-CUCUMBER RELISH

Serves 4

Chicken thighs work well on the barbecue because they have more fat than the ubiquitous chicken breasts and, when cooked, are juicier and far more flavorful. If you don't have an outdoor grill, this recipe can be made year-round using a stove-top ridged griddle pan. The marinade also works with pork, prawns, or turkey and the relish, which keeps, covered and refrigerated, for up to 3 days, is great with almost anything you can imagine, from roasts to barbecues.

250 ml (8 fl oz) unsweetened coconut milk

2 tablespoons sesame oil

2 tablespoons finely chopped spring onion

1 tablespoon chopped mint leaves

1 tablespoon sesame seeds

1 tablespoon lime juice

8 small bone-in, skin-on chicken thighs (about 675 g/1 lb 8 oz total weight)

Salt and pepper

125 ml (4 fl oz) Jicama-Cucumber Relish (recipe follows)

Combine the coconut milk with the sesame oil, spring onion, mint, sesame seeds, and lime juice in a large resealable plastic bag. Add the chicken, seal, and roll around to evenly coat. Refrigerate for at least 1 hour or up to 12 hours.

Preheat and oil the barbecue or alternatively heat a nonstick stove-top griddle pan.

Remove the chicken from the bag and season with salt and pepper to taste. Place on the hot barbecue (or preheated griddle pan) and grill, turning frequently, for about 12 minutes or until just cooked through. Do not overcook or the meat will be dry and tough.

Remove from the grill and transfer to a serving platter. Serve with the relish on the side.

Nutritional Analysis per Serving: calories 412, carbohydrates 4 g, fiber 1 g, protein 24 g, fat 34 g, sodium 296 mg, sugar 0 g.

JICAMA-CUCUMBER RELISH

Makes about 550 ml (18 fl oz)

125 g (4½ oz) jicama, peeled and finely chopped

200 g (7 oz) cucumber, seeded and finely chopped

4 tablespoons chopped mint leaves

2 tablespoons chopped spring onion

1 teaspoon freshly grated orange zest

3 tablespoons white vinegar

½ teaspoon stevia

Salt

Combine the jicama, cucumber, mint, spring onion, and orange zest in a small mixing bowl. Add the vinegar and stevia. Season with salt to taste and stir to combine. Cover and refrigerate for 30 minutes to allow flavors to blend. The relish may be stored, covered and refrigerated, for up to 3 days.

Nutritional Analysis per Serving (2 tablespoons): calories 3, carbohydrates 1 g, fiber 0 g, protein 0 g, fat 0 g, sodium 49 mg, sugar 0 g.

NOTE: Jicama is a bulbous root vegetable with white crunchy flesh, popular in Mexican cooking. Water chestnuts or white radish (mooli) could be substituted.

CHICKEN WITH 40 CLOVES OF GARLIC

Serves 4

This is a classic dish from Provence. I wonder if the original cook labeled it with the 40 cloves of garlic to scare future cooks off from this unique recipe. Interestingly, the garlic mellows as it cooks and becomes quite sweet; some cooks use up to 100 cloves. The resulting sauce is buttery and mildly fragrant and takes everyday chicken to new heights.

3 tablespoons avocado oil, plus more for greasing pan

1.6 kg (3 lb 8 oz) roasting chicken, cut into 8 pieces

Salt and pepper

40 cloves garlic, peeled

75 ml (3 fl oz) dry vermouth

1 teaspoon dried tarragon

175 ml (6 fl oz) Chicken Stock (see page 33) or low-sodium, nonfat chicken stock

1 teaspoon lemon juice

1 tablespoon chopped chives

Preheat the oven to 200ºC/400ºF/Gas Mark 6.

Heat the oil in a large, heavy-bottom saucepan over medium heat.

Lightly coat the interior of a small roasting pan with avocado oil. Set aside.

Season the chicken with salt and pepper to taste and add it to the saucepan, skin side down. Sear, turning occasionally, for about 12 minutes or until nicely browned on all sides. Using tongs, transfer the chicken to the roasting pan. Leave the saucepan on the heat.

Place all of the garlic in the saucepan and cook, stirring frequently, for about 5 minutes or just until it begins to brown. Add the vermouth and tarragon and cook, scraping up the browned bits from the bottom of the pan, for about 4 minutes or until reduced by half.

Add the stock, raise the heat, and bring to a boil. Boil for about 5 minutes or just until the garlic has softened. Using a slotted spoon, transfer 10 of the garlic cloves to the roasting pan. Using a kitchen fork, mash the remaining garlic cloves into the liquid in the saucepan.

Pour the sauce over the chicken and transfer to the preheated oven.

Roast for about 20 minutes or until the chicken is cooked through and the sauce is thick and flavorful.

Remove from the heat and transfer the chicken to a serving platter. Add the lemon juice to the sauce, stirring to blend. Taste and, if necessary, season with additional salt and pepper. Pour the sauce over the chicken and garnish with chives.

Serve immediately.

Nutritional Analysis per Serving: calories 574, carbohydrates 9 g, fiber 1 g, protein 53 g, fat 33 g, sodium 588 mg, sugar 2 g.

CHICKEN BREASTS STUFFED WITH SWISS CHARD AND GOAT CHEESE

Serves 4

Company coming? Put this wonderful recipe together early in the day and pop it in the oven while drinks are served. Dinner will be on the table in minutes without you spending much time in the kitchen at all.

If Swiss chard is not available, use leaf spinach or kale, and the goat cheese can be replaced with any soft cheese you like.

1 tablespoon extra virgin olive oil

1 shallot, peeled and finely chopped

225 g (8 oz) Swiss chard, tough stems removed and finely
   chopped

Salt and pepper

1 teaspoon freshly grated orange zest

4 x 140-g (5-oz) boneless, skin-on chicken breasts

115 g (4 oz) soft goat cheese

25 g (1 oz) butter, melted

Preheat the oven to 200ºC/400ºF/Gas Mark 6.

Heat the oil in a large frying pan over medium-low heat. Add the shallot and cook, stirring frequently, for about 2 minutes or until soft. Add the chard and season with salt and pepper to taste. Cook, stirring occasionally, for about 5 minutes or until the chard has wilted and any liquid has evaporated.

Remove from the heat and stir in the orange zest. Set aside to cool.

Working with one breast at a time and using a small sharp knife, cut a pocket into the chicken by cutting into the center but not through the entire breast. Begin at the thickest end and continue the length of the breast until you have a deep pocket. Season the pockets with salt and pepper.

When the chard has cooled, crumble the goat cheese and toss it into the chard. Using your fingers, fill each pocket with an equal portion of the chard/cheese mixture. Close the pockets by sticking a couple of cocktail sticks into the edge.

Generously coat the exterior of each breast with melted butter and season with salt and pepper to taste.

Place the stuffed breasts into a small roasting pan. Transfer to the preheated oven and bake for about 15 minutes or until the meat is cooked through and the skin golden brown.

Remove from the oven and serve.

Nutritional Analysis per Serving: calories 382, carbohydrates 6 g, fiber 1 g, protein 37 g, fat 24 g, sodium 596 mg, sugar 3 g.

JERK CHICKEN

Serves 6

This is as close to an outdoor vendor on a Jamaican beach as you can get in your own backyard (or kitchen). Blisteringly hot, spicy, and juicy is just what you'll get here.

You can make as much of the seasoning as you like as it will keep, covered and refrigerated, for up to 1 month. Jamaicans prefer their seasoning to be made with lots and lots of fresh Scotch Bonnet chillies, which are extremely hot. You can create the amount of heat you desire by adding or decreasing the amount of fresh chilli. Just remember you are looking for the perfect balance of heat, spice, and acid.

125 ml (4 fl oz) lime juice

2 tablespoons white vinegar

2 tablespoons finely chopped hot chilli, such as Scotch Bonnet, or
   to taste

1 tablespoon freshly grated orange zest

2 tablespoons mustard seeds

1 tablespoon dried thyme

1 tablespoon ground allspice

1 teaspoon ground cloves

$\frac{1}{2}$ teaspoon ground nutmeg

Salt and pepper

6 bone-in, skin-on chicken thighs

1 lime, cut into wedges, optional

Combine the lime juice and vinegar in the jar of a blender. Add the chilli and orange zest and process to blend. Then add the mustard, thyme, allspice, cloves, and nutmeg. Process to a thick sauce-like consistency. If too thick, add additional citrus juice or vinegar.

Preheat and oil the barbecue.

Lightly coat each thigh with the spice mixture and season with salt and pepper to taste. Place on the outer rim of the grill slightly away from direct heat, skin side down, cover, and grill for about 10 minutes or until they are crisp and almost cooked through. Turn and continue to grill for an additional 8 minutes or until the chicken is thoroughly cooked. If you don't have a barbecue available, the chicken may be cooked in a stove-top ridged griddle pan or in a preheated 190ºC/375ºF/Gas Mark 5 oven for about the same amount of time.

Remove from the grill and serve with wedges of lime, if desired.

VARIATIONS This seasoning is excellent on any type of chicken or turkey, pork chops, pork fillet, whole fish, or fish fillets.

Nutritional Analysis per Serving: calories 349, carbohydrates 3 g, fiber 1 g, protein 31 g, fat 23 g, sodium 312 mg, sugar 0 g.

BAKED CHICKEN PARCELS

Serves 4

This is a super dish for entertaining as the little parcels can be put together in advance and baked just before serving. In this case, make the parcels from parchment paper as it is a bit more attractive at the table than foil. This recipe can also be used with firm white fish, such as halibut.

4 x 140-g (5-oz) boneless, skinless chicken breasts

2 teaspoons chopped basil

1 teaspoon chopped thyme

8 pieces sun-dried tomato packed in oil, well-drained

2 tablespoons sliced black or green Greek olives

4 rosemary sprigs

25 g (1 oz) unsalted butter

Salt and pepper

1 tablespoon chia seeds

Tear 4 pieces of aluminium foil large enough to completely enclose a chicken breast – they will probably need to be about 30 cm (12 inches) or so long. If using parchment paper, cut 4 pieces of paper into a heart shape about 30 cm (12 inches) long.

Preheat the oven to 180ºC/350ºF/Gas Mark 4.

If using foil, lay the 4 pieces out on the counter. Place a chicken breast in the center of each one. Season each breast with equal amounts of basil and thyme. Criss-cross 2 pieces of sun-dried tomato on top of each piece of chicken. Add a few slices of olives over each. Lay a sprig of rosemary on top. Place equal pats of butter on top and season with salt and pepper to taste. Finally sprinkle chia seeds over all. Roll the foil up and around the chicken to tightly seal the foil and completely enclose the chicken.

If using parchment paper, place the breast on one side of the heart shape near the center and layer the ingredients on top, as above. Pull the paper up and over the chicken so each side meets. Starting at one end of the half heart, begin folding the edges in and over to make a tight seal as you work your way around to firmly enclose the chicken. If desired, you can wet the inner edge of the paper with a bit of egg white before folding it over the chicken to ensure a tight seal.

Place the parcels in a baking dish in the preheated oven and bake for about 20 minutes or until the chicken is cooked through and aromatic.

Serve the individual parcels to be opened at the table.

VARIATIONS Rather than in parcels, the recipe may be made in a slow cooker. You will need to add 4 tablespoons of chicken stock or water and cook on low for about 3 hours. Any herb or spice can be used at your discretion, and the sun-dried tomatoes can easily be replaced with fresh peeled and chopped plum tomatoes.

Nutritional Analysis per Serving: calories 235, carbohydrates 4 g, fiber 2 g, protein 30 g, fat 11 g, sodium 527 mg, sugar 1 g.

CHICKEN CURRY WITH CORIANDER CHUTNEY

Serves 4

This has all the flavors of South Asian cooking without the work of making an authentic curry. If you choose to use it, the toasted flaked coconut will add a touch of sweetness and crunch to offset the heat. The chutney is cooling, and the green makes an inviting contrast to the vibrant orange curry. Steamed Cauliflower Couscous (see page 133) would make a fabulous base for the curry as it would absorb much of the tasty sauce.

450 g (1 lb) skinless, boneless chicken breasts and/or thighs, cut
    into bite-sized pieces

Salt

Cayenne pepper

15 g (1/2 oz) ghee or butter

225 g (8 oz) onion, peeled and finely chopped

1 teaspoon finely chopped garlic

2 teaspoons hot curry powder

1/2 teaspoon turmeric

250 ml (8 fl oz) Chicken Stock (see page 33) or low-sodium
    chicken stock, plus more if needed

125 ml (4 fl oz) unsweetened coconut milk

85 g (3 oz) water chestnuts, sliced

175 g (6 oz) chopped frozen spinach, well-drained

3 tablespoons toasted coconut flakes, optional

4 tablespoons Coriander Chutney (recipe follows), optional

Season the chicken with salt and cayenne pepper to taste.

Heat the ghee in a large, nonstick frying pan over medium heat. Add the chicken and cook, stirring frequently, for about 4 minutes or just until it begins to color. Remove the chicken from the pan and set aside.

Add the onion, garlic, curry powder, and turmeric to the pan, stirring to combine. Cook, stirring constantly, for about 3 minutes or just until the onion has wilted.

Return the chicken to the pan and add the stock and coconut milk. Taste and, if necessary, add additional salt and cayenne. Stir in the water chestnuts and spinach, cover, and cook for about 12 minutes or until the chicken has cooked through and the sauce has thickened.

Remove from the heat and, if desired, serve sprinkled with toasted coconut flakes and the chutney passed on the side.

Nutritional Analysis per Serving (includes 1 tablespoon chutney): calories 279, carbohydrates 11 g, fiber 3 g, protein 25 g, fat 15 g, sodium 149 mg, sugar 3 g.

CORIANDER CHUTNEY

Makes about 300 ml (½ pint)

1 large bunch coriander, tough stems removed, well washed and
   dried

½ yellow pepper, seeded and chopped

4 tablespoons chopped mint leaves

3 tablespoons chopped fresh coconut

1 teaspoon chopped hot green chilli or to taste

½ teaspoon chopped ginger root

Grilled Parmesan Tomatoes (page 124)

London Broil with Grilled Mushrooms (page 140)

Grilled Pork Chops with Salsa Verde (page 165)

Barbecued Coconut-Sesame Chicken with Jicama-Cucumber Relish (page 175)

Garlic Prawns (page 206)

Salmon Roasted in Butter and Almonds (page 192)

Cauliflower "Hummus" (page 238)

Vegetable Crisps (page 224)

Chocolate Almond Cake (page 247)

Raw Chia Seed Pudding
(page 253)

Coconut Bursts
(page 243)

1 tablespoon lemon juice

1 teaspoon toasted ground cumin

Salt

Combine the coriander, yellow pepper, mint, coconut, chilli, and ginger in the bowl of a food processor fitted with a metal blade. Process, using quick on and off turns, until finely chopped.

Scrape the mixture into a serving bowl. Add the lemon juice, cumin, and salt and stir to combine.

Serve immediately or cover and store, refrigerated, for up to 1 day.

Nutritional Analysis per Serving (1 tablespoon): calories 7, carbohydrates 1 g, fiber 0 g, protein 0 g, fat 0 g, sodium 61 mg, sugar 0 g.

CHICKEN WITH LEMON AND OLIVES

Serves 4

Although I use a quartered chicken, you can cook Cornish hens, chicken pieces, or pork chops in this style. The sauce that results during baking is sweet, sour, and salty; a perfect accent to the mild chicken. Do note that the lemons should be eaten along with the meat. They become quite tender and mellow as they cook.

1.6 kg (3 lb 8 oz) chicken, cut into quarters

75 ml (3 fl oz) extra virgin olive oil

4 tablespoons white wine

2 lemons, cut into quarters

175 g (6 oz) Kalamata olives

2 tablespoons chopped mint leaves

1 tablespoon chopped thyme

1 tablespoon chopped sage

Salt and pepper

Preheat the oven to 200ºC/400ºF/Gas Mark 6.

Place the chicken in a large baking dish and pour in the olive oil and wine. Nestle the lemons around the chicken. Then, sprinkle the olives, mint, thyme, and sage over all. Season with salt and pepper to taste, noting that the olives will add some saltiness to the mix.

Cover and transfer to the preheated oven. Roast for 30 minutes; then lower the oven temperature to 180ºC/350ºF/Gas Mark 4 and continue to roast for another 20 minutes or until the chicken is golden brown and cooked through.

Remove from the oven and transfer the chicken to a serving platter. Spoon the lemons and olives around the chicken and pour the pan sauce into a gravy boat. Serve immediately or at room temperature.

Nutritional Analysis per Serving: calories 661, carbohydrates 3 g, fiber 1 g, protein 52 g, fat 47 g, sodium 629 mg, sugar 0 g.

SESAME CHICKEN

Serves 4

Rather than the expected coating of breadcrumbs or flour, sesame seeds create an amazingly crisp crust. The butter/lemon quick sauce isn't necessary but it adds a little zip to the finished dish. For extra zest, add some garlic or ginger to the melting butter.

8 thin boneless skinless chicken breasts (about 565 g/1 lb 4 oz
    total weight)
Salt and pepper
200 g (7 oz) sesame seeds
3 tablespoons avocado oil
75 g (2³/₄ oz) butter
Juice of 1 lemon

Season the chicken with salt and pepper.

Place the sesame seeds in a large shallow bowl. Working with one piece at a time, carefully coat both sides of the chicken breasts with sesame seeds.

Heat the oil in a large frying pan over medium heat. Add the chicken and fry, turning once, for 8 minutes or until golden brown and cooked through.

Transfer the chicken to a serving platter.

Wipe the oil from the pan and return the pan to medium heat. Add the butter and swirl it around to melt. Stir in the lemon juice and when combined pour the sauce over the chicken. Serve immediately.

Nutritional Analysis per Serving: calories 697, carbohydrates 5 g, fiber 2 g, protein 42 g, fat 57 g, sodium 381 mg, sugar 0 g.

HERB-ROASTED TURKEY BREAST
Serves 6

Although terrific on the dinner table, this turkey breast is perfect for out-of-hand snacking at any time of the day. The herb coating adds just the right amount of zesty flavor to the meat. If you are used to supermarket turkey, you can expect a heritage traditional turkey to have deeper flavor and darker meat.

1 half turkey breast, bone-in

60 g (2 oz) butter, at room temperature

8 tablespoons chopped mixed herbs, such as flat-leaf parsley, tarragon, chives, basil

Salt and pepper

250 ml (8 fl oz) Chicken Stock (see page 33) or low-sodium chicken stock

Preheat the oven to 220ºC/425ºF/Gas Mark 7.

Using your hands, pat the butter onto the turkey skin. Place the herbs on a clean, flat surface and roll the buttered side of the turkey on them. You want to completely coat the skin. Season with salt and pepper to taste.

Place the seasoned turkey breast in a small roasting pan. Add the stock to the pan and place in the preheated oven.

Roast for about 30 minutes or until an instant-read thermometer inserted into the thickest part registers 70ºC/160ºF.

Remove from the oven and let rest for about 10 minutes before slicing.

Cut into slices, crosswise, and serve with the pan juices drizzled over the top.

Nutritional Analysis per Serving: calories 214, carbohydrates 1 g, fiber 0 g, protein 32 g, fat 8 g, sodium 456 mg, sugar 0 g.

TURKEY STEAKS WITH ROASTED PEPPERS AND CHEESE

Serves 4

This dish takes no time and little effort to put together, but it is nonetheless delicious. An amazing combination of textures and flavors take this dish far, far away from the standard Thanksgiving bird. If you don't have homemade tapenade on hand – which you should – commercially jarred will work just fine, as long as it is carb-free.

4 x 115-g (4-oz) turkey steaks

1 tablespoon avocado oil

Salt and pepper

4 roasted red pepper halves

4 tablespoons Tapenade (see page 42)

115 g (4 oz) pepper jack or Cheddar cheese, grated

Preheat the grill.

Generously rub the steaks with avocado oil and season with salt and pepper to taste.

Preheat a stove-top ridged griddle pan. When hot, add the steaks and grill, turning occasionally, for about 8 minutes or until cooked through and nicely marked.

Remove from the griddle pan and place in a baking tin with sides small enough to fit under the grill. Lay one half of each roasted pepper on top of each steak. Drizzle a little tapenade over the top and then generously cover with the cheese.

Place under the preheated grill and grill for about 3 minutes or until the cheese has melted and is bubbly and lightly colored.

Remove from the oven and serve.

Nutritional Analysis per Serving: calories 333, carbohydrates 6 g, fiber 2 g, protein 36 g, fat 18 g, sodium 622 mg, sugar 3 g.

SPICY TURKEY MEATBALLS IN TOMATO SAUCE

Serves 4

Although scented with Italy by the basil and cheese, you can easily change the flavor of these meatballs by eliminating those Italian favorites and adding other herbs and/or spices that reflect other cultures. If you are not a fan of heat, just eliminate the cayenne and you will still have very tasty meatballs. Whatever you do, just remember to match the flavors of the tomato sauce to the flavors of the meat.

450 g (1 lb) minced turkey

30 g (1 oz) pecorino romano cheese, grated

55 g (2 oz) onion, peeled and finely chopped

1 tablespoon chopped flat-leaf parsley

3 tablespoons chopped basil or 1½ teaspoons dried basil

Salt

Cayenne pepper

1 large egg

3 tablespoons extra virgin olive oil

1 tablespoon finely chopped garlic

2 x 400-ml (14-oz) cans chopped tomatoes

Black pepper

Crushed chilli flakes, optional

Combine the minced turkey with the grated cheese, onion, and parsley. Add 1 tablespoon of the basil along with salt and cayenne to taste. Add the egg and, using your hands, thoroughly blend the mixture together.

Using your hands, form the turkey into balls about 2.5 cm (1 inch) in diameter.

Heat 2 tablespoons of the oil in a large frying pan over medium-high heat. Add the meatballs and fry, turning frequently, for about 10 minutes or until nicely browned and cooked through.

Remove the meatballs from the pan and place on a double layer of kitchen paper to drain.

Heat the remaining 1 tablespoon of olive oil in a large nonreactive saucepan over medium heat. Add the garlic and cook, stirring, for about 2 minutes or just until slightly softened. Add the tomatoes and remaining basil and season with salt and pepper to taste and, if using, chilli flakes.

Add the meatballs and bring to a simmer. Lower the heat and cook at a gentle simmer for 15 minutes.

VARIATIONS These meatballs can be made with minced chicken, pork, or beef.

Nutritional Analysis per Serving: calories 489, carbohydrates 17 g, fiber 5 g, protein 34 g, fat 32 g, sodium 580 mg, sugar 5 g.

FISH AND SHELLFISH

Salmon Roasted in Butter and Almonds

Salmon in Chilli Broth

Salmon Burgers with Herbed Tartar Sauce

Slow-Roasted Salmon with Mustard Glaze

Mint-Coconut Salmon

Herb-Grilled Halibut Steaks

Grilled Trout with Brown Butter

Whole Roasted Sea Bream

Ginger-Glazed Mahi Mahi

Fillet of Sole in Champagne Sauce

Portuguese-Style Sardines

Garlic Prawns

Prawn Creole

Cioppino

SALMON ROASTED IN BUTTER AND ALMONDS

Serves 4

Salmon, butter, and almonds – what could be better? If you can, do garnish with the cracked pepper. It offers just a hint of heat to balance the fatty fish and the buttery sauce.

675 g (1 lb 8 oz) skin-on salmon fillet

Salt and pepper

85 g (3 oz) butter

75 g (2¾ oz) flaked almonds

1 tablespoon lemon juice

2 tablespoons chopped chives

Cracked black pepper for garnish, optional

Preheat the oven to 240°C/475°F/Gas Mark 9.

Season the salmon with salt and pepper. Set aside.

Place the butter and almonds in a small baking dish in the preheated oven. When the butter has melted, add the salmon, flesh side down. Roast for 5 minutes; then, turn and continue to roast for another 3 minutes or until the salmon is beginning to barely flake. (You can test by sticking the point of a small, sharp knife into the flesh to see if it flakes or easily comes apart.)

Remove from the oven and transfer the salmon to a serving platter. Stir the lemon juice and chives into the "sauce" in the pan and immediately pour over the salmon. Sprinkle with cracked black pepper, if desired, and serve.

Nutritional Analysis per Serving: calories 602, carbohydrates 5 g, fiber 3 g, protein 42 g, fat 46 g, sodium 377 mg, sugar 1 g.

SALMON IN CHILLI BROTH

Serves 4

This is a light dish to serve any time of the year. If you are not a fan of salmon – or have had too many salmon dinners – use any other meaty fish you like; halibut or grouper would make a more than acceptable substitute.

500 ml (17 fl oz) bottled clam juice

1 small hot green chilli, stemmed and cut, crosswise, into thin slices

2 teaspoons anchovy paste

1 teaspoon tahini

1 teaspoon lime juice

1 teaspoon finely sliced ginger root

4 x 175-g (6-oz) skin-on salmon fillets

1 teaspoon almond oil

Salt

450 g (1 lb) tiny broccoli florets

1 tablespoon chopped chives

1 teaspoon black sesame seeds, optional

Preheat the oven to 190ºC/375ºF/Gas Mark 5.

Combine the clam juice with the chilli, anchovy paste, tahini, lime juice, and ginger in a medium saucepan over medium heat. Cover and bring to a simmer. Simmer for 5 minutes or just long enough to allow the flavors to blend. Uncover, but leave on the stove.

Lightly brush the salmon with the oil and season with salt. Place the fish, skin side down, in an ovenproof frying pan over high heat. Sear for about 4 minutes or just until the skin is crisp and the salmon has begun to cook. Turn and transfer to the preheated oven. Bake for an additional 4 minutes or until the fish is cooked to medium.

While the fish is in the oven, add the broccoli to the broth and cook over medium heat for about 3 minutes or until still bright green, but slightly cooked.

Ladle an equal portion of the broth and broccoli into each of 4 shallow soup bowls.

Remove the fish from the oven and, using a spatula, place one fillet in the center of each bowl. Sprinkle chives and, if using, black sesame seeds over all and serve.

Nutritional Analysis per Serving: calories 237, carbohydrates 3 g, fiber 1 g, protein 36 g, fat 8 g, sodium 681 mg, sugar 1 g.

SALMON BURGERS WITH HERBED TARTAR SAUCE

Serves 4

A bit more interesting than the old-fashioned salmon croquettes, these burgers would make an inviting party dish served on a bed of sautéed greens. You don't absolutely need the tartar sauce, but it adds that little touch of sour that complements the richness of the salmon.

450 g (1 lb) chopped fresh salmon

1 large egg yolk

4 tablespoons finely diced red or yellow pepper

4 tablespoons almond meal

2 tablespoons Dijon mustard

1 tablespoon chopped chives

Salt and white pepper

About 1 tablespoon ghee

125 ml (4 fl oz) Herbed Tartar Sauce (recipe follows)

Preheat the grill and oil the grill pan or preheat a stove-top ridged griddle pan.

Combine the salmon, egg yolk, diced pepper, almond meal, mustard, and chives and season with salt and white pepper.

Form the mixture into 4 patties of equal size.

Using a pastry brush, coat both sides of the patties with the ghee. Place under the grill (or in the griddle pan) and grill for 4 minutes. Turn and grill for another 5 minutes or until cooked through. Remove from the heat and serve with the tartar sauce on the side.

Nutritional Analysis per Serving (includes 2 tablespoons tartar sauce): calories 284, carbohydrates 5 g, fiber 1 g, protein 25 g, fat 18 g, sodium 481 mg, sugar 1 g.

HERBED TARTAR SAUCE

Makes about 250 ml (8 fl oz)

3 green olives

4 tablespoons cornichons (see Note)

1 shallot, peeled and chopped

1 hard-boiled egg yolk

1 teaspoon chopped capers

1 teaspoon chopped flat-leaf parsley

1 teaspoon chopped chives

1 teaspoon chopped dill

125 ml (4 fl oz) Mayonnaise (see page 38)

1 teaspoon Dijon mustard

Salt and pepper

Combine the olives, cornichons, shallot, egg yolk, capers, parsley, chives, and dill in the bowl of a food processor fitted with a metal blade. Process, using quick on and off turns, until coarsely chopped. Add the mayonnaise and mustard and process to blend. Taste and, if necessary, season with additional salt and pepper.

Scrape from the processor bowl into a clean container, cover, and refrigerate until ready to use. May be stored, covered and refrigerated, for up to 3 days.

NOTE Cornichons are small French pickles that are available from specialty food stores, many supermarkets, or online.

Nutritional Analysis per Serving (2 tablespoons): calories 55, carbohydrates 1 g, fiber 0 g, protein 0 g, fat 6 g, sodium 95 mg, sugar 0 g.

SLOW-ROASTED SALMON WITH MUSTARD GLAZE

Serves 4

Slowly roasting this dish gives the buttery glaze time to shine and allows the salmon to remain moist and flavorful. The heat of the mustard is the perfect balance for the sweet, fatty fish. A side of a peppery watercress salad or Green Beans with Walnuts (see page 135) would complete the meal.

85 g (3 oz) unsalted butter, softened, plus more for greasing the
    dish
4 tablespoons finely ground almonds
2 tablespoons chopped flat-leaf parsley
2 teaspoons Dijon mustard
1 teaspoon mustard seeds
1 teaspoon freshly grated lemon zest
4 x 140-g (5-oz) skinless salmon fillets
Salt and pepper

Preheat the oven to 140°C/275°F/Gas Mark 1.

Generously butter a shallow baking dish large enough to hold the fish without crowding.

Place the butter in a small mixing bowl. Add the almonds, parsley, mustard, mustard seeds, and lemon zest and, using a rubber spatula, knead to blend thoroughly.

Using a table knife spread an equal portion of the butter mixture over the top of each piece of salmon. Season with salt and pepper to taste and then transfer to the baking dish.

Place in the preheated oven and roast for about 20 minutes or just until the fish is barely cooked through and the top is glazed.

Remove from the oven and serve.

Nutritional Analysis per Serving: calories 313, carbohydrates 2 g, fiber 1 g, protein 30 g, fat 20 g, sodium 279 mg, sugar 0 g.

MINT-COCONUT SALMON

Serves 4

The barely cooked slaw is the perfect accent to the moist, coconut-flavored salmon. Combining the vegetables and the protein in one package helps bring dinner to the table in a snap. The extra benefit is that the parcels can be put together a couple of hours in advance of cooking and popped into the oven at the last minute for a stress-free meal.

115 g (4 oz) green cabbage, shredded

4 tablespoons finely diced red pepper

1 tablespoon shredded unsweetened coconut

1 tablespoon chopped mint leaves plus more for garnish

2 teaspoons chopped coriander

1 teaspoon lime juice

Salt and pepper

4 x 140-g (5-oz) salmon fillets

75 ml (3 fl oz) unsweetened coconut milk

2 tablespoons toasted coconut flakes

Preheat the oven to 180ºC/350ºF/Gas Mark 4.

Cut 4 pieces of parchment paper into a heart shape about 30 cm (12 inches) long. Set aside.

Toss the cabbage with the red pepper, coconut, mint, coriander, and lime juice. Season with salt and pepper to taste.

Place a mound of seasoned cabbage on one side of the heart shape near the center. Season the fish with salt and pepper to taste and then lay a piece on top of the cabbage in each package. Drizzle coconut milk over the top and pull the paper up and over the salmon so each side meets. Starting at one end of the half heart, begin folding the edges in and over to make a tight seal as you work your way around to firmly enclose cabbage and salmon. If desired, you can wet the inner edge of the paper with a bit of egg white before folding it over the salmon to ensure a tight seal.

Place the parcels in a baking dish in the preheated oven and bake for about 12 minutes or until the salmon is just barely cooked through and very aromatic.

Serve the individual parcels to be opened at the table with a sprinkle of toasted coconut and chopped mint leaves, if desired.

Nutritional Analysis per Serving: calories 247, carbohydrates 5 g, fiber 2 g, protein 29 g, fat 12 g, sodium 229 mg, sugar 2 g.

HERB-GRILLED HALIBUT STEAKS

Serves 4

Fresh herbs make all the difference in this recipe, giving a lighter, cleaner flavor than dried. However, if you don't have them on hand, don't hesitate to replace them with dried herbs, remembering that you will require substantially less as the flavor of the dried herbs is more intense. The herb-crusted fish looks absolutely delectable served with Healthy Green Slaw (see page 108), Sautéed Cherry Tomatoes and Herbs (see page 125), or Radishes Braised in Butter (see page 121).

4 tablespoons chopped thyme

4 tablespoons chopped oregano

4 tablespoons chopped flat-leaf parsley

Cayenne pepper

Salt and pepper

4 tablespoons coconut oil

4 x 140-g (5-oz) 2-cm ($^3/_4$-inch) thick halibut steaks

Preheat the grill and oil the grill pan or preheat a stove-top ridged griddle pan.

Combine the thyme, oregano, and parsley in a shallow bowl. Season with cayenne, salt, and pepper to taste, tossing to blend well.

Using a pastry brush, generously coat both sides of the halibut steaks with coconut oil. Press both sides of the fish into the herb mixture, pushing down to coat well.

Place the steaks under the grill or in the preheated griddle pan. Grill, turning only once, for about 12 minutes or until the fish is just barely cooked through.

Remove from the heat and serve.

Nutritional Analysis per Serving: calories 413, carbohydrates 2 g, fiber 1 g, protein 22 g, fat 35 g, sodium 415 mg, sugar 0 g.

GRILLED TROUT WITH BROWN BUTTER

Serves 4

Effortless and classic – what more could a cook want? This is a piece of cake to put together and always makes a strong impression. You can, if you wish, add about 4 tablespoons flaked almonds to the butter as it is browning for an extra *Grain Brain* hit.

115 g (4 oz) unsalted butter

1 teaspoon lemon juice

1 tablespoon chopped flat-leaf parsley

1 teaspoon chopped chives

Salt and white pepper

4 whole trout, cleaned

Melt the butter in a small frying pan over low heat. Cook, stirring frequently, for about 3 minutes or until it begins to foam. Continue to cook slowly until it turns golden brown and the aroma is very nutty, taking care that it doesn't burn. Remove from the heat and stir in the lemon juice, parsley, and chives. Season with salt and white pepper to taste. Set aside and keep warm while the fish grills.

Preheat the grill and oil the grill pan or preheat a stove-top ridged griddle pan over medium-high heat.

Season the trout with salt and pepper to taste. Place under the hot grill (or in the hot griddle pan) and grill for 4 minutes. Carefully turn (preferably with a fish slice) to keep the fish whole, and grill for another 5 minutes or until cooked through.

Remove from the grill and serve with the butter drizzled over the top.

Nutritional Analysis per Serving: calories 450, carbohydrates 0 g, fiber 0 g, protein 35 g, fat 33 g, sodium 378 mg, sugar 0 g.

WHOLE ROASTED SEA BREAM

Serves 4

Nothing like a fresh-from-the-ocean whole fish cooked simply. I either roast the fish in a hot oven or do a quick turn on the grill – either way it is deliciously moist. This recipe can be used for almost any firm-fleshed fish or thick fillets of meaty fish such as halibut. Roasting whole fish at a high temperature seals in its juices so it remains extremely moist.

2 x 1.1–1.4 kg (2½–3 lb) sea bream, cleaned, head and tail intact

1 lemon, well washed and cut, crosswise, into thin slices plus more
    for optional garnish

8 sprigs dill plus more for garnish, if desired

8 sprigs flat-leaf parsley plus more for garnish, if desired

3 tablespoons avocado oil

Salt and pepper

2 large bulbs fennel, cut, crosswise, into thin slices

2 onions, peeled and cut, crosswise, into thin slices

2 tablespoons chopped fennel fronds

Preheat the oven to 230ºC/450ºF/Gas Mark 8.

Rinse the fish and pat dry, both inside and out. Layer the lemon slices in the cavity of each fish. Place 4 sprigs each of dill and parsley in each cavity. Using your hands, generously coat the fish with the oil and season both sides with salt and pepper.

Combine the fennel and onions with the chopped fennel fronds in a shallow roasting pan large enough to hold both of the fish. Season with salt and pepper to taste and push the vegetables out to an even layer. Pour 125 ml (4 fl oz) water into the pan and then place the fish on top of the vegetables.

Place in the preheated oven and roast, turning the vegetables occasionally, for about 30 minutes or until the vegetables are tender and an instant-read thermometer inserted into the thickest part of the fish reads 58ºC/135ºF.

Remove the pan from the oven and allow the fish to rest for 5 minutes before serving.

Using two spatulas, carefully lift each fish from the roasting pan onto a serving platter. Spoon the fennel-onion mixture around the fish and, if desired, garnish with chopped dill or parsley and additional lemon slices.

Nutritional Analysis per Serving: calories 289, carbohydrates 7 g, fiber 2 g, protein 35 g, fat 13 g, sodium 392 mg, sugar 4 g.

GINGER-GLAZED MAHI MAHI

Serves 4

The key to this recipe is the preheating of the oven before baking the fish, as a very hot oven will cook the fish quickly and create an attractive glazed coating. If you can't find lemongrass replace it with about a teaspoon of lemon zest. The flavor will be a bit more intense, but it will be just fine. A notable partner for the mahi mahi would be the Jicama-Cucumber Relish on page 176.

2 stalks lemongrass, white part only, chopped

2 tablespoons finely chopped coriander

1 tablespoon grated ginger root

1 tablespoon coconut oil

1 tablespoon balsamic vinegar

Salt and pepper

4 x 140-g (5-oz) mahi mahi fillets

About 20 minutes before ready to cook, preheat the oven to 230ºC/450ºF/Gas Mark 8.

Combine the lemongrass, coriander, ginger, coconut oil, vinegar, and salt and pepper to taste in a small mixing bowl.

Using your fingertips, spread the mixture over one side of the fish fillets and let marinate for 10 minutes.

Place the fish in a nonstick ovenproof pan, coated-side up. Transfer to the preheated oven and roast for about 5 minutes or just until the fish is barely cooked and the coating has glazed.

Remove from the oven and serve.

Nutritional Analysis per Serving: calories 191, carbohydrates 2 g, fiber 0 g, protein 34 g, fat 5 g, sodium 307 mg, sugar 1 g.

FILLET OF SOLE IN CHAMPAGNE SAUCE

Serves 4

This is a classic French dish that was once very popular in four-star restaurants but is rarely seen anymore. It is quick to put together, rich, and delicious, and when served in individual gratin dishes makes a stunning presentation at the table.

115 g (4 oz) plus 40 g (1½ oz) unsalted butter, at room
  temperature

125 ml (4 fl oz) Chicken Stock (see page 33) or low-sodium
  chicken stock

4 tablespoons bottled clam juice

450 g (1 lb) sole fillets or other delicate white fish fillets

225 g (8 oz) small prawns, peeled and deveined

12 shucked oysters, well-drained

4 tablespoons champagne or other sparkling white wine

4 large egg yolks, beaten, at room temperature

Salt and white pepper

1 tablespoon chopped chives

Preheat the oven to 160ºC/325ºF/Gas Mark 3.

Using 40 g (1½ oz) of the butter, generously coat the interior of a shallow baking dish large enough to hold the fish or 4 individual gratin dishes.

Combine the chicken stock and clam juice. Set aside.

Arrange the fish fillets in a single layer over the bottom of the dish. Pour 4 tablespoons of the clam juice/chicken stock mix over the top. Place the prawns and oysters over the fish. Cover the dish with aluminium foil without allowing the foil to touch the fish.

Place in the preheated oven and bake for 15 minutes or just until the fish is cooked through.

While the fish is cooking, place the remaining clam juice/chicken stock mix in the top half of a double boiler placed over high heat. Bring to a boil and boil until reduced by half.

Remove from the heat and place the top half of the double boiler over the bottom half that has been filled with boiling water. Whisk in the champagne and when hot, whisk in the remaining 115 g (4 oz) butter until emulsified.

Place the egg yolks in a small mixing bowl. Whisking constantly beat about 4 tablespoons of the hot mixture into the yolks. When well blended, beating constantly, add the tempered egg yolks to the hot mixture in the top of the double boiler. Return the entire double boiler to high heat, season the sauce with salt and white pepper, and continue to cook, whisking constantly, for 5 minutes or until the sauce is smooth and thick.

Remove the fish from the oven and preheat the grill.

Uncover the fish and pour the sauce over the top. Place under the grill and grill for 3 minutes or until bubbling and golden brown.

Remove from the grill, sprinkle with chopped chives, and serve.

Nutritional Analysis per Serving: calories 492, carbohydrates 4 g, fiber 0 g, protein 27 g, fat 39 g, sodium 815 mg, sugar 0 g.

PORTUGUESE-STYLE SARDINES

Serves 4

Only in recent years have fresh sardines been available in America, after nutritionists began promoting their health benefits. Unlike many other fish, sardines still seem to be abundant and they are rich in protein, one of the most concentrated sources of the omega-3 fatty acids EPA and DHA, high in vitamins B12 and D, and fatty and delicious. They can be cooked simply on the grill and served with just a squeeze of lemon, with any number of sauces, or in this delightful Portuguese-style recipe.

4 tablespoons extra virgin olive oil

8 large sardines, cleaned

1 medium onion, peeled and cut, lengthwise, into thin slices

1 tablespoon finely chopped garlic

1 red pepper, cored, seeded, membrane removed, and cut, lengthwise, into thin slices

600 g (1 lb 5 oz) very ripe tomatoes, diced, with their juice

1 bay leaf

$\frac{1}{2}$ teaspoon saffron

4 anchovies packed in oil, chopped

Preheat the oven to 200ºC/400ºF/Gas Mark 6.

Using 1 tablespoon of the oil, generously coat the interior of a baking dish large enough to hold the fish in a single layer. Place the fish in the dish and set aside.

Heat the remaining 3 tablespoons of oil in a large frying pan over medium heat. Add the onion and garlic and cook, stirring occasionally, for 5 minutes. Add the red pepper and continue to cook, stirring occasionally, for about 6 minutes or until the onion and pepper are nicely colored.

Stir in the tomatoes along with the bay leaf and saffron. Bring to a simmer and simmer for 5 minutes. Then, pour the tomato mixture over the fish and season with salt and pepper to taste. Dot the top of the dish with the chopped anchovies.

Transfer to the preheated oven and bake for 20 minutes or until the fish is cooked through and the sauce aromatic.

Remove from the oven and serve hot or at room temperature.

Nutritional Analysis per Serving: calories 410, carbohydrates 10 g, fiber 3 g, protein 31 g, fat 28 g, sodium 446 mg, sugar 6 g.

GARLIC PRAWNS

Serves 4

This is my version of a dish that on Italian menus is known as "scampi." It is usually served with lots of bread, but I think it more than stands on its own. Like almost every protein, scampi works well with a side of sautéed greens. Cook prawns very briefly or you'll have chewy little monsters.

85 g (3 oz) unsalted butter or ghee

4 tablespoons finely chopped garlic

4 tablespoons dry white wine

3 tablespoons lemon juice

450 g (1 lb) large raw prawns, peeled and deveined

Salt and pepper

2 tablespoons finely chopped flat-leaf parsley

Heat the butter in a large frying pan over medium heat. Add the garlic and cook, stirring, for about 2 minutes or just until soft, but not colored.

Stir in the wine and lemon juice and when blended, add the prawns. Season with salt and pepper to taste and bring to a simmer. Simmer for about 2 minutes or just until the prawns are firm and pink. Do not overcook or the prawns will be tough.

Remove from the heat and stir in the parsley. Serve immediately.

NOTE For those on a restricted sodium diet, just be aware that prawns, alone, are quite high in sodium and you might want to substitute chunks of a firm white fish in its place.

Nutritional Analysis per Serving: calories 281, carbohydrates 5 g, fiber 0 g, protein 20 g, fat 18 g, sodium 819 mg, sugar 0 g.

PRAWN CREOLE

Serves 4

This recipe will take you down on the bayou with just a few minutes in the kitchen. If you don't have Creole seasoning on hand, you can make your own by combining 1 tablespoon each of dried thyme and oregano, onion and garlic powders, and black pepper with 2 tablespoons salt, paprika, and cayenne.

2 tablespoons extra virgin olive oil

225 g (8 oz) onions, peeled and diced

75 g (2³/₄ oz) red pepper, finely diced

75 g (2³/₄ oz) green pepper, finely diced

1 tablespoon finely chopped garlic

1 tablespoon Creole seasoning

1 tablespoon tomato purée

500 ml (17 fl oz) canned chopped tomatoes without their juice

250 ml (8 fl oz) bottled clam juice

Pepper

450 g (1 lb) prawns, peeled and deveined

1 tablespoon chopped flat-leaf parsley

Heat the oil in a large frying pan over medium heat. Add the onions, peppers, and garlic and cook, stirring frequently, for about 5 minutes or until the vegetables begin to soften. Stir in the Creole seasoning and tomato purée and cook for another minute. Add the tomatoes and clam juice and bring to a simmer. Taste and, if necessary, add pepper.

Simmer for about 20 minutes or until the flavors are well blended. Add the prawns and return to the simmer. Cook for 3 minutes or just until the prawns are cooked through.

Remove from the heat, stir in the parsley, and serve.

Nutritional Analysis per Serving: calories 202, carbohydrates 10 g, fiber 2 g, protein 21 g, fat 9 g, sodium 892 mg, sugar 4 g.

CIOPPINO

Serves 6

Cioppino is a traditional San Francisco shellfish stew created by early Italian settlers who fished the local waters. It is similar to all Mediterranean fish stews in that you can make it with almost any combination of fish and shellfish and in any base, although tomato is almost always the defining flavor. This recipe only uses shellfish but you can easily replace most of the shellfish with fin fish. It is up to you to make it everything you want an aromatic stew to be.

125 ml (4 fl oz) extra virgin olive oil

4 large cloves garlic, sliced

1 large onion, chopped

1 carrot, very finely chopped

1 bulb fennel, cleaned, trimmed, and cut, lengthwise, into thin slices

125 ml (4 fl oz) dry red wine

4 x 400-ml (14-oz) cans chopped Italian plum tomatoes with their
   juice

250 ml (8 fl oz) clam juice

2 tablespoons chopped basil leaves

2 tablespoons chopped flat-leaf parsley plus more for garnish, if
   desired

Salt and pepper

1 to 2 large crabs, cracked into pieces

2 dozen clams

2 dozen mussels

Heat the olive oil in a large saucepan over medium heat. Add the garlic, onion, carrot, and fennel and cook, stirring frequently, for about 5 minutes or until the vegetables begin to soften. Add the wine and cook for about 5 minutes or until most of the alcohol has burned off.

Stir in the tomatoes and their juices along with the clam juice.

Bring to a simmer. Stir in the basil and parsley and season with salt and pepper to taste. Cook at a low simmer for 15 minutes or until the flavors have blended nicely.

Add the crab pieces, clams, and mussels. Cover and cook for about 10 minutes or until the shellfish is cooked and the shells have opened.

Ladle into individual shallow soup bowls or one large soup tureen. Garnish with additional parsley and serve.

Nutritional Analysis per Serving: calories 425, carbohydrates 23 g, fiber 5 g, protein 33 g, fat 22 g, sodium 821 mg, sugar 9 g.

MEATLESS

Baked Aubergine, Courgette, and Tomato
Chillies Stuffed with Goat Cheese
Baked Spaghetti Squash with Tomato Sauce
and Parmesan Cheese
Sautéed Courgette "Noodles" with Butter and Cheese

BAKED AUBERGINE, COURGETTE, AND TOMATO

Serves 4

This is an all-year-round casserole that sings of the south of France and hints at a touch of Italy. It can be made early in the day and baked just before dinner. It is terrific at room temperature, too, which makes it perfect for a leftover lunch.

4 tablespoons extra virgin olive oil plus more for greasing the dish

1 large aubergine, trimmed and cut, crosswise, into 5-mm ($\frac{1}{4}$-inch) thick slices

4 courgettes, trimmed and cut, lengthwise, into 5-mm ($\frac{1}{4}$-inch) thick slices

Salt and pepper

125 ml (4 fl oz) Tomato Sauce (see page 37)

5 ripe tomatoes, peeled, cored, and cut, crosswise, into thin slices

4 tablespoons torn basil leaves

340 g (12 oz) mozzarella cheese, grated

25 g (1 oz) Parmesan cheese, grated

Preheat the oven to 230ºC/450ºF/Gas Mark 8.

Line 2 baking sheets with parchment paper. Set aside.

Lightly coat the interior of a 20-cm (8-inch) baking dish with olive oil. Set aside.

Cut each aubergine slice in half. Using a pastry brush, lightly coat both sides of the aubergines and courgettes with olive oil. Place the vegetables on the prepared baking sheets and season with salt and pepper to taste. Place in the preheated oven and bake for about 12 minutes or until just barely cooked and lightly browned. Remove from the oven and set aside to cool.

Lower the oven temperature to 180ºC/350ºF/Gas Mark 4.

Ladle the Tomato Sauce into the prepared baking dish. Using half of the aubergine slices place a layer of aubergine over the sauce. Then, top the aubergine with half of the courgettes, laying the courgettes in the opposite direction from the aubergine. Using half of the tomatoes, cover the courgettes. Sprinkle half of the basil over the tomatoes and season with salt and pepper to taste. Then sprinkle half of the mozzarella over the seasoned tomatoes, making an even layer. Continue making layers so that you end with a layer of cheese. Sprinkle the top with Parmesan and transfer to the preheated oven.

Bake for about 30 minutes or until hot throughout and the cheese has melted and browned slightly.

Remove from the oven and let rest for 10 minutes before cutting into squares and serving.

Nutritional Analysis per Serving: calories 538, carbohydrates 25 g, fiber 7 g, protein 26 g, fat 40 g, sodium 559 mg, sugar 13 g.

CHILLIES STUFFED WITH GOAT CHEESE

Serves 4

It takes a little work to make these chillies, but the time and effort is well worth the result. Not at all spicy, stuffed chillies are wonderfully delicious and deserve to be on the table frequently. If you can't find the chillies called for in the recipe, you can use almost any other chilli, or green peppers.

4 roasted red peppers, stemmed, seeded, and membrane removed

2 tablespoons extra virgin olive oil

1 teaspoon balsamic vinegar

1½ teaspoons ground toasted cumin

Salt

½ teaspoon Tabasco sauce or to taste

4 fresh New Mexico green or fresh Anaheim chillies

115 g (4 oz) mild goat cheese

25 g (1 oz) pepper jack or Cheddar cheese, coarsely grated

4 tablespoons chopped oil-packed sun-dried tomatoes, well
   drained

3 large eggs

About 4 tablespoons coconut oil for frying

Combine the roasted red peppers with the oil and vinegar in the bowl of a food processor fitted with the metal blade. Add 1 teaspoon of the cumin and process to a smooth purée. Scrape into a mixing bowl and season with salt and Tabasco. Cover and set aside.

Preheat the grill.

Place the chillies on a grill pan under the hot grill and grill, turning occasionally, for about 7 minutes or until nicely charred, but not completely blackened. Remove from the heat and immediately place in a resealable plastic bag or a container with a tight lid. Seal or cover and allow to sweat for 15 minutes or until the skin has begun to loosen from the flesh.

Remove the chillies and, working with one at a time, carefully push off the charred skin. Work gently as you don't want to tear the chillies.

Using a small, sharp knife, slit each chilli, lengthwise down one side. Carefully pull back the flesh and remove and discard the seeds. Set aside.

Combine the goat cheese, jack cheese, sun-dried tomatoes, and remaining 1/2 teaspoon cumin in the bowl of a food processor fitted with a metal blade and process until smooth.

Place the chillies on a clean, flat work surface and working with one at a time, carefully spoon an equal portion of the cheese mixture into the opening, using just enough cheese to fill the cavity yet still allow the chilli to close around it. Use your fingers to lightly press the edges of the chilli together.

Separate the eggs.

Place the egg yolks in a medium mixing bowl. Add ¼ teaspoon salt and, using a whisk, beat until light.

Place the white in the bowl of a standing electric mixer and beat on high until stiff peaks form. Remove the bowl from the mixer and slowly fold the beaten egg yolks into the whites. Continue folding until only a few lines of egg yolk are evident.

Heat the oil in a deep frying pan large enough to hold all of the chillies over medium-high heat.

Working with one chilli at a time, carefully dip the chilli into the beaten egg whites. Do not press on the chilli or the stuffing will pop out. This is most easily done by holding the chilli on a large perforated spatula and dipping it in and out of the egg.

Carefully lay the chillies into the hot oil and fry, turning once, for about 4 minutes or until the coating is golden brown and slightly crisp.

Remove from the oil and place on a double layer of kitchen paper to drain quickly.

Ladle about 5 tablespoons of the roasted pepper sauce onto the center of each of 4 serving plates. Lay a stuffed chilli in the center and serve immediately as the chillies will get soggy quickly.

Nutritional Analysis per Serving: calories 316, carbohydrates 15 g, fiber 4 g, protein 14 g, fat 24 g, sodium 285 mg, sugar 10 g.

BAKED SPAGHETTI SQUASH WITH TOMATO SAUCE AND PARMESAN CHEESE

Serves 4

Spaghetti squash really can take the place of flour-based pastas. Once you get the hang of roasting it and pulling the flesh out in strands you will see what I mean. You can use it with any type of sauce that you would normally use for pasta, even the classic Italian cacio e pepi (cheese and pepper) would make a sublime meal.

Since this dish is relatively high in carbohydrates, take care about the remainder of your total carbohydrate intake for the day.

1 large (about 2.3 kg/5 lb) spaghetti squash

1 tablespoon plus 2 teaspoons extra virgin olive oil

160 g (5¼ oz) button mushrooms, coarsely chopped

1 small onion, peeled and chopped

1 teaspoon finely chopped garlic

1 serving of Tomato Sauce (see page 37)

Salt and pepper

1 tablespoon chopped basil

55 g (2 oz) Parmesan cheese, grated

Preheat the oven to 190ºC/375ºF/Gas Mark 5.

Using a sharp knife, cut the squash in half, lengthwise. Using a spoon, carefully scoop out the seeds. Either discard the seeds or set them aside to dry out and roast at a later time (see page 255).

Place the squash, cut side down, in a 23 x 33 cm (9 x 13 inch) baking tin. Add 1 tablespoon of the olive oil along with 4 tablespoons water to the tin. Transfer to the preheated oven and bake for about 30 minutes or until very tender when pierced with the end of a small, sharp knife.

Remove the squash from the oven (do not turn the oven off) and turn it cut side up. Using a kitchen fork, carefully scrape the stringy flesh from the skin in long spaghetti-like strands.

Lightly coat the interior of a 20-cm (8-inch) square baking dish with 1 teaspoon of olive oil. Mound the spaghetti squash in the dish and set aside.

Heat the remaining 1 teaspoon of olive oil in a large frying pan over medium heat. Add the mushrooms, onion, and garlic and cook, stirring, for about 15 minutes or until the mushrooms are nicely browned. Add the Tomato Sauce and continue to cook for 20 minutes. Taste and, if necessary, season with additional salt and pepper. Stir in the basil and remove from the heat.

THE GRAIN BRAIN COOKBOOK

Spoon the sauce over the squash. Top with Parmesan cheese, transfer to the oven, and bake for about 15 minutes or until the top is lightly browned and the squash is very hot.

Remove from the oven and serve.

Nutritional Analysis per Serving: calories 336, carbohydrates 44 g, fiber 10 g, protein 13 g, fat 15 g, sodium 615 mg, sugar 18 g.

SAUTÉED COURGETTE "NOODLES" WITH BUTTER AND CHEESE

Serves 4

It's not spaghetti, but it sure tastes better. The nutty brown butter and the salty cheese turn the mild courgettes into something supreme. You do need a julienne peeler to get the long strands necessary, but they are inexpensive and you can purchase one at most large supermarkets or kitchen shops or, of course, online.

900 g (2 lb) (about 6) yellow and green courgettes, trimmed, but
   not peeled
115 g (4 oz) butter
Salt and pepper
85 g (3 oz) Parmesan cheese, grated
40 g (1½ oz) rocket, finely chopped

Working with one courgette at a time and using a julienne vegetable peeler, begin at one end and pull the peeler all the way down the length to make long spaghetti-like strands. Continue making strands until all of the courgettes have been cut.

Place the butter in a large frying pan over medium heat and let it cook until it just begins to brown. Add the courgette strands, season with salt and pepper to taste, and cook, tossing and turning with tongs, until just barely tender and well coated with brown butter.

Remove from the heat and toss in the cheese and rocket. Taste and, if necessary, season with additional salt and pepper.

Serve immediately.

Nutritional Analysis per Serving: calories 350, carbohydrates 7 g, fiber 2 g, protein 12 g, fat 29 g, sodium 674 mg, sugar 5 g.

SNACKS

A couple of snacks during the day can add diversity to your diet, and any of these will more than accomplish that. Some of these recipes take no effort, some create a batch that will see you through the week, some work as a side dish, and some make fabulous special occasion treats. All of them would make outstanding party and entertaining fare and, believe me, your guests will be none the wiser that they have been snacking on "good-for-you" foods.

Roast Pumpkin or Squash Seeds
Crunchy Pumpkin Seed Toss
Kale Crisps
Vegetable Crisps
Curried Almonds
French-Fried Almonds
Chilli Nuts
Deviled Nuts
Spiced Cheese Pot
Saganaki
Marinated Olives
Deviled Eggs
Chicken Liver Pâté
Artichoke Dip
Celery Stuffed with Cashew Butter
Chicory Leaves with Caponata

Stuffed Mushrooms
Marinated Almond Mushrooms
Cauliflower "Hummus"
Aubergine-Walnut Dip

ROAST PUMPKIN OR SQUASH SEEDS

Makes whatever amount your pumpkin or squash yields

Waste not, want not, the old saying goes. Many of us throw out the seeds we scrape from pumpkins and squashes when they can easily be turned into terrifically healthy snack food. When baking the seeds, you can add any herb or spice you like – about 1 teaspoon ground spice should be enough to season the seeds from one pumpkin.

Seeds from 1 pumpkin or other hard-skinned squash, such as
 butternut
2 tablespoons extra virgin olive oil or coconut or avocado oil
Salt, optional

Preheat the oven to 150ºC/300ºF/Gas Mark 2.

Line a roasting tray with parchment paper. Set aside.

Using your fingertips, clean off any pieces of flesh clinging to the seeds. Place the seeds in a colander under cold running water and rinse thoroughly to remove any stringy pieces of flesh remaining.

Transfer the seeds to a double layer of kitchen paper to drain. Using more kitchen paper, pat off any water that remains.

Place the seeds on the prepared roasting tray. Add the oil and, if using, salt to taste, tossing to coat. Be sure that the seeds are in a single layer so that they will roast evenly.

Transfer to the preheated oven and roast, stirring occasionally, for about 25 minutes or until the seeds are beginning to turn golden brown.

Remove from the oven and set aside to cool completely before storing, tightly covered, at room temperature for up to 5 days.

Nutritional Analysis per Serving (2 tablespoons): calories 293, carbohydrates 5 g, fiber 1 g, protein 11 g, fat 26 g, sodium 7 mg, sugar 0 g.

CRUNCHY PUMPKIN SEED TOSS

Makes about 16 tablespoons

This is a zesty seed/nut mix that makes a perfect afternoon snack. You can easily triple the amount of seeds and nuts and still use the same amount of egg and spice. This mix is also a wonderful garnish on vegetables or grilled chicken or fish.

50 g (1³/₄ oz) pumpkin seeds

4 tablespoons raw cashews

4 tablespoons sunflower seeds

2 tablespoons chia seeds

2 large egg whites, at room temperature

1 teaspoon curry powder

¹/₄ teaspoon cayenne pepper

Pinch turmeric

Pinch stevia

Salt

Preheat the oven to 150ºC/300ºF/Gas Mark 2.

Line a roasting tray with parchment paper. Set aside.

Combine the pumpkin seeds with the cashews, sunflower seeds, and chia seeds in a medium mixing bowl. Set aside.

Place the egg whites in a small mixing bowl. Whisk in the curry powder, cayenne, turmeric, and stevia. Whisk until very frothy.

Pour the egg white mixture over the seeds and nuts and toss to coat well. Using a slotted spoon, transfer the mixture to the prepared roasting tray, taking care to allow excess egg white to drop off. Transfer to the preheated oven and bake, turning occasionally, for about 30 minutes or until golden brown and crisp.

Remove from the oven and season with salt. Let cool before serving or storing, airtight at room temperature, for up to 1 week.

Nutritional Analysis per Serving (2 tablespoons): calories 293, carbohydrates 5 g, fiber 1 g, protein 11 g, fat 26 g, sodium 7 mg, sugar 0 g.

KALE CRISPS

Makes 4 servings

Kale crisps didn't exist a couple of years ago, but now you find them in stores all across the country. You can easily make them yourself and have them on hand to snack on all through the day. They are a terrific alternative to commercial crisps, potato or otherwise. You can actually bake any leafy green in this same fashion. It is impossible to tell how many crisps you will yield as kale bunches vary in size and, in addition, it will depend upon how large you cut the leaves.

1 large bunch kale, tough stems removed and cut into large pieces
3 tablespoons extra virgin olive oil or coconut oil
Salt

Preheat the oven to 150ºC/300ºF/Gas Mark 2.
Line 2 roasting trays with parchment paper. Set aside.
Place the kale in a large mixing bowl. Add the oil and salt, to taste, and toss to coat well. Spread the kale on the prepared roasting trays in a single layer. Transfer to the preheated oven and bake for about 8 minutes or until the kale begins to brown. Using tongs, turn the kale and continue to bake for an additional 12 minutes or until brown, crisp, and crackly.

Remove from the oven and season with additional salt, if desired. Serve immediately or store, tightly covered, at room temperature for up to 3 days. If the chips lose their crunch, reheat in a 140ºC/275ºF/ Gas Mark 1 oven for 5 minutes.

Nutritional Analysis per Serving: calories 132, carbohydrates 8 g, fiber 2 g, protein 4 g, fat 11 g, sodium 178 mg, sugar 0 g.

VEGETABLE CRISPS

Suggested serving 24 pieces

Far better than commercial potato crisps, but just as addictive! The crisps will keep for a week or so if stored, airtight, at room temperature. Along with salt you can season them with pepper, cayenne, ground herbs, and/or spices. You can use one or all of the following vegetables to make crisps. It's up to you to make your own variety.

1 large beetroot, peeled

1 celeriac, peeled

1 swede, peeled

1 lotus or taro root, peeled

450 g (1 lb) Jerusalem artichokes, well scrubbed

1 jicama, peeled

1 large carrot, peeled

Beef dripping, extra virgin olive oil, or coconut or avocado oil for deep-frying

Salt

Using a Japanese vegetable slicer or a mandoline and working with one vegetable at a time, slice the vegetables into potato-crisp-thin slices. As sliced, dry well with kitchen paper as any moisture will dilute the hot oil and affect the ability of the vegetable to brown quickly.

Heat the oil in a deep-fat fryer (or a deep saucepan) over medium-high heat to 180ºC/350ºF on a sugar thermometer.

Fry the vegetable slices a few at a time so that they don't stick together. Fry for about 1 minute or until lightly colored and crisp.

Using either the fryer basket or a slotted spoon, transfer the crisps to a double layer of kitchen paper to drain.

Season with salt and serve.

Nutritional Analysis per Serving (24 pieces): calories 60, carbohydrates 7 g, fiber 2 g, protein 1 g, fat 4 g, sodium 74 mg, sugar 2 g.

CURRIED ALMONDS

Makes 565 g (1 lb 4 oz)

These are not one bit difficult to make and offer more excitement than having a handful of plain, unblanched almonds for a snack. Chopped, they make an excellent garnish on grilled poultry or fish.

565 g (1 lb 4 oz) blanched almonds

115 g (4 oz) butter

1 tablespoon hot curry powder

2 teaspoons garlic salt or to taste

Preheat the oven to 150ºC/300ºF/Gas Mark 2.

Linea roasting tray with parchment paper.

Place the almonds on the prepared tray in a single layer. Transfer to the preheated oven and roast for about 25 minutes or until golden brown.

Place the butter in a small saucepan over medium heat. Add the curry powder and garlic salt and cook, stirring, for about 3 minutes or until melted and aromatic.

Pour the butter mixture over the baked almonds, tossing to coat well, and continue to bake, stirring occasionally, for an additional 15 minutes or until well coated and glazed.

Remove from the oven and, using a slotted spoon, transfer the almonds to a double layer of kitchen paper to drain.

When drained and cool, store, tightly covered at room temperature, for no more than 10 days.

Nutritional Analysis per Serving (6 pieces): calories 44, carbohydrates 2 g, fiber 1 g, protein 2 g, fat 4 g, sodium 24 mg, sugar 0 g.

FRENCH-FRIED ALMONDS

Makes 450 g (1 lb)

With this recipe, you have to make sure that you fry the almonds long enough to get them crisp but not burned. This can happen very quickly so watch carefully as you cook.

150 ml (¼ pint) coconut oil

450 g (1 lb) unblanched almonds

Seasoned salt

Heat the oil in a large frying pan over medium-high heat. When melted, lower the heat and add the almonds. Fry, stirring frequently, for about 7 minutes or until the almonds are brown and crispy.

Using a slotted spoon, transfer the almonds to a double layer of kitchen paper to drain.

When drained, sprinkle with salt and allow to cool.

Serve immediately or store, tightly covered at room temperature, for up to 10 days.

Nutritional Analysis per Serving (6 pieces): calories 212, carbohydrates 7 g, fiber 4 g, protein 7 g, fat 19 g, sodium 83 mg, sugar 1 g.

CHILLI NUTS

Makes 900 g (2 lb)

If you like, you can add some seeds, such as pumpkin or sunflower, to this mix. Again, watch carefully as the nuts cook so that they reach the perfect degree of golden goodness without a hint of char.

225 g (8 oz) raw cashews

225 g (8 oz) raw pecans

225 g (8 oz) raw walnuts

225 g (8 oz) pistachios

75 g (2³/₄ oz) butter, melted

1 tablespoon chilli powder

¹/₂ teaspoon cayenne pepper

¹/₂ teaspoon garlic salt

Preheat the oven to 150ºC/300ºF/Gas Mark 2.

Line 2 large roasting trays with parchment paper. Place the nuts on the prepared trays in a single layer. Transfer to the preheated oven and roast, stirring occasionally, for about 25 minutes or until golden brown.

Combine the melted butter with the chilli powder, cayenne, and garlic salt and pour the mixture over the hot nuts, tossing to coat. Continue to roast, stirring frequently, for an additional 15 minutes or until shiny golden brown and crisp.

Remove from the oven and, using a slotted spoon, transfer to a double layer of kitchen paper to drain and cool.

Serve immediately or store, tightly covered at room temperature, for up to 10 days.

Nutritional Analysis per Serving (6 pieces): calories 190, carbohydrates 6 g, fiber 2 g, protein 5 g, fat 17 g, sodium 16 mg, sugar 2 g.

DEVILED NUTS

Makes 450 g (1 lb)

Smoke and spice is what you get with this nut combo. These are great for snacking or for passing around with a glass of red wine at cocktail time. This recipe may also be used with pumpkin seeds.

40 g (1¹/₂ oz) ghee or butter

450 g (1 lb) mixed roasted unsalted nuts, such as cashews, almonds, hazelnuts, walnuts, and/or pecans

Dash of Worcestershire sauce

1½ teaspoons salt

¼ teaspoon cayenne pepper

¼ teaspoon smoked paprika

¼ teaspoon chilli powder

⅛ teaspoon ground cumin

Heat the ghee in a large frying pan over medium heat. Add the nuts and fry, stirring frequently, for about 5 minutes or until golden. Add a dash of Worcestershire sauce and stir to blend.

Remove from the heat and, using a slotted spoon, transfer to a double layer of kitchen paper to drain.

When well drained, place in a resealable plastic bag along with the salt, cayenne, paprika, chilli powder, and cumin. Seal and shake vigorously to evenly coat the nuts with the spices.

Pour out onto a clean baking sheet and set aside to cool. When cool, serve or store, tightly covered at room temperature, for up to 10 days.

Nutritional Analysis per Serving (6 pieces): calories 219, carbohydrates 6 g, fiber 3 g, protein 6 g, fat 20 g, sodium 251 mg, sugar 1 g.

SPICED CHEESE POT

Makes about 750 ml (1¼ pints)

Rather than just a plain hunk of cheese for a snack, try this slightly spicy mix. It is particularly good spooned on a lettuce or chicory leaf or packed into a celery stick for an afternoon pick-me-up.

450 g (1 lb) mature Cheddar cheese, grated

75 ml (3 fl oz) coconut oil

3 tablespoons finely chopped shallot or onion

2 tablespoons finely chopped chives

1 tablespoon Dijon mustard

1 teaspoon hot curry powder

½ teaspoon cayenne pepper

Combine the cheese, coconut oil, shallot, chives, mustard, curry powder, and cayenne in the bowl of a food processor fitted with a metal blade. Process until smooth.

Scrape from the processor bowl into a clean container and store, tightly covered and refrigerated, for up to 2 weeks.

Nutritional Analysis per Serving (2 tablespoons): calories 103, carbohydrates 1 g, fiber 0 g, protein 5 g, fat 9 g, sodium 137 mg, sugar 0 g.

SAGANAKI

Makes 450 g (1 lb)

Saganaki is a traditional Greek meze or appetizer/snack. It is often served after being flamed with ouzo, a Greek liqueur, on the stove or at the table. The name comes from the pan, a *sagani*, in which the cheese is usually fried. The oil has to be very hot so that the cheese browns quickly before it melts completely. Saganaki is often part of an appetizer table served with tomatoes, olives, and, in Greece, lots of bread. Normally dusted with flour, I find that the delicate almond flavor adds a lovely accent to the slightly acidic cheese.

65 g (2¼ oz) almond meal

450 g (1 lb) halloumi, kefalotyri, or kasseri cheese (or pecorino
    romano or feta)

125 ml (4 fl oz) extra virgin olive oil

Quartered lemon for serving

Place the almond meal in one shallow bowl and about 500 ml (17 fl oz) cold water in another.

Using a sharp knife, cut the cheese into pieces that are about 1 cm

(½ inch) thick and 7.5 cm (3 inches) wide. Working with one piece at a time, dip into the cold water, allowing excess water to drip off. Then, dredge in the almond meal, again allowing excess to fall off.

Heat the olive oil in a large frying pan over medium heat. Add the cheese and fry, turning once, for about 2 minutes or until golden and crusty on both sides.

Remove from the heat and serve with a spritz of lemon juice.

Nutritional Analysis per Serving (1 piece): calories 245, carbohydrates 3 g, fiber 1 g, protein 14 g, fat 24 g, sodium 603 mg, sugar 0 g.

MARINATED OLIVES

Makes 225 g (8 oz)

You can make as many of these aromatic olives as you like; however, it is easier to make and store them in 250-ml (8 fl oz) containers. I suggest pitted olives only for their convenience, but you can use those with pits if you like and, of course, if you are partial to a particular type of olive, by all means use it.

    225 g (8 oz) pitted mixed olives
    2 cloves garlic, peeled and sliced
    1 dried chilli
    1 small sprig rosemary
    Extra virgin olive oil
    Red wine vinegar

Place half of the olives in a 250-ml (8 fl oz) container. Add the garlic, chilli, and rosemary and cover with the remaining olives. Fill the container two-thirds full with the oil and top off with the vinegar. Cover and shake vigorously to mix.

Store, tightly covered and refrigerated, for at least 2 days before using. Then, store, covered and refrigerated, for up to 1 month.

Nutritional Analysis per Serving (6 olives): calories 90, carbohydrates 3 g, fiber 0 g, protein 1 g, fat 9 g, sodium 642 mg, sugar 0 g.

DEVILED EGGS

Makes 24

If you go to the trouble of making Deviled Eggs, you might as well start with a dozen eggs because everyone loves them and they will disappear faster than you can imagine. If you want to get fancy, add finely chopped prawns, crab meat, or anchovies to the yolks and garnish with a tiny parsley or coriander leaf. Or add some chopped flat-leaf parsley, mint, basil, or coriander to the mix to vary the flavor for everyday eggs.

12 hard-boiled eggs, peeled

4 tablespoons Mayonnaise (see page 38)

1 tablespoon Dijon mustard or more to taste

Pinch cayenne pepper

White vinegar, optional

Salt and pepper

Paprika for garnish, optional

Cut the eggs in half, lengthwise, carefully keeping each half in one piece. Gently remove the yolks and place them in a small mixing bowl. Set the whites aside.

Combine the egg yolks with the mayonnaise, mustard, and cayenne pepper. Using a kitchen fork, mash the mixture together. If the mixture seems too dry, add a bit more mayo or mustard or a couple of drops of vinegar. Season with salt and pepper to taste.

Either scrape the mixture into a piping bag fitted with a small star nozzle and carefully pipe an equal portion of the mashed yolk mixture into each white half, mounding slightly, or simply portion the yolk mixture into the white using a teaspoon to mound slightly. Lightly dust with paprika.

Serve immediately or cover lightly with clingfilm and refrigerate until ready to use or for no longer than 8 hours.

Nutritional Analysis per Serving (2 halves): calories 167, carbohydrates 2 g, fiber 0 g, protein 10 g, fat 14 g, sodium 229 mg, sugar 1 g.

CHICKEN LIVER PÂTÉ

Makes about 500 g (1 lb 2 oz)

Pâtés make superb snacking treats as they are filling and extremely nutritious. This one is uncomplicated to make and keeps well either refrigerated for up to 1 week or frozen for up to 6 weeks. If you are storing for more than a day or so, melt about 4 tablespoons of butter and pour it over the pâté. Once the butter hardens the top is sealed and the pâté remains fresh. You don't have to scrape the butter off when serving; it simply becomes part of the pâté.

225 g (8 oz) chicken livers, well trimmed

115 g (4 oz) onion, peeled and chopped

½ teaspoon chopped garlic

1 bay leaf

¼ teaspoon chopped sage

¼ teaspoon chopped thyme

Salt

1 tablespoon dry sherry

175 g (6 oz) butter, at room temperature

Pepper

Combine the chicken livers with the onion, garlic, bay leaf, sage, and thyme in a medium saucepan over medium-low heat. Add 125 ml

(4 fl oz) water along with salt and bring to a simmer. Cover, lower the heat, and cook for about 5 minutes or until the livers are just barely cooked. Remove from the heat and set aside for 5 minutes.

Uncover, remove and discard the bay leaf. Pour the liver mixture into a fine mesh strainer set over a mixing bowl, discarding the liquid.

Transfer the drained liver mixture to the bowl of a food processor fitted with a metal blade. Add the sherry and process until chopped. With the motor running, begin adding the butter, a bit at a time, processing until all of the butter has been incorporated and the pâté is completely smooth. Season with salt and pepper to taste.

Scrape the mixture into a serving bowl, smoothing down the top until even. Place a piece of clingfilm directly on the pâté and place in the refrigerator to chill until very firm.

When ready to serve, remove the pâté from the refrigerator, uncover, and serve with celery, red pepper, cucumber sticks, or chicory leaves.

Nutritional Analysis per Serving (2 tablespoons): calories 82, carbohydrates 1 g, fiber 0 g, protein 3 g, fat 7 g, sodium 72 mg, sugar 0 g.

ARTICHOKE DIP

Makes about 500 ml (17 fl oz)

Artichoke dip came into its own in the 1960s, and there have been iterations of it for almost every generation since then. There are two *Grain Brain* versions – one cold and one hot – and both are deliciously healthy and work equally well with raw vegetables. The cold one is fine for everyday dipping and the hot for an appetizer or hors d'oeuvre when company's coming.

Cold

1 x 425-g (15-oz) can artichoke hearts, well drained

125 ml (4 fl oz) Mayonnaise (see page 38)

1 tablespoon chopped basil, flat-leaf parsley, or chives

Salt and pepper

Place the artichoke hearts in the bowl of a food processor fitted with a metal blade. Add the mayonnaise and herbs, season with salt and pepper to taste, and process until almost smooth. You want to see a little texture in the mix.

Scrape from the processor into a serving bowl and serve with raw vegetables for dipping.

Hot

1 quantity Cold Artichoke Dip

285 g (10 oz) frozen chopped spinach or kale, thawed and well
   drained

1 teaspoon finely chopped garlic

85 g (3 oz) Parmesan cheese, grated

50 g (1¾ oz) mozzarella cheese, grated

Preheat the oven to 180°C/350°F/Gas Mark 4.

Generously coat the interior of a 23-cm (9-inch) round baking dish or pie plate with butter. Set aside.

Combine the cold dip with the spinach and garlic, stirring to blend well. Add two-thirds of the Parmesan cheese along with the mozzarella and again stir to blend well. Taste and, if necessary, add salt and pepper.

Scrape the mixture into the prepared baking dish, smoothing the top with a rubber spatula. Sprinkle the remaining Parmesan over the top. Transfer to the preheated oven and bake for about 20 minutes or until cooked through and golden brown on the top.

Remove from the oven and serve with raw vegetables for dipping.

Nutritional Analysis for Cold Dip per Serving (2 tablespoons): calories 67, carbohydrates 5 g, fiber 1 g, protein 1 g, fat 6 g, sodium 188 mg, sugar 2 g.

Nutritional Analysis for Hot Dip per Serving (2 tablespoons): calories 227, carbohydrates 11 g, fiber 3 g, protein 9 g, fat 16 g, sodium 610 mg, sugar 4 g.

CELERY STUFFED WITH CASHEW BUTTER

Makes 16 pieces

This is a new take on that old childhood favorite, peanut-butter-stuffed celery. These celery sticks will keep, tightly covered and refrigerated, for about 3 days. You can make the cashew butter mix and keep it on hand to make a stuffed celery stick whenever the snacking mood hits. If you are feeling ambitious, store the mix in a piping bag fitted with a star nozzle and run a star-shaped line down the celery groove as the spirit moves you.

175 g (6 oz) cashew butter

85 g (3 oz) soft goat cheese

1 teaspoon freshly grated orange zest

Tabasco sauce or to taste

16 medium ribs celery, trimmed and chilled

4 tablespoons chopped toasted cashews, optional

Combine the cashew butter, goat cheese, orange zest, and Tabasco in the bowl of a food processor fitted with a metal blade. Process until well blended and very smooth.

Using a kitchen knife, spread an equal portion of the cashew butter mix down the groove in each piece of celery. If desired, sprinkle chopped cashews on top and serve.

Nutritional Analysis per Serving (1 stick): calories 97, carbohydrates 5 g, fiber 1 g, protein 3 g, fat 7 g, sodium 54 mg, sugar 2 g.

CHICORY LEAVES WITH CAPONATA

Makes as many as you would like

You can, if you like, speed things up with commercially prepared caponata or ratatouille as the filling, IF they are fine quality with no carb or gluten content. But, since I know you always have Caponata (see page 105) on hand, this could be an everyday snack. The recipe couldn't be simpler. One head of chicory will yield quite a few leaves, but they will, for the most part, be of varying sizes, so a tablespoon on one large leaf might look a bit skimpy, but then on a small leaf it might just ooze over the top. Since you are snacking, it shouldn't matter.

For each large chicory leaf you will need 1 tablespoon Caponata (see page 105)

Trim the bottom edge from the chicory leaf. Spoon the Caponata in the center and snack.

Nutritional Analysis per Serving (1 large leaf): calories 93, carbohydrates 10 g, fiber 3 g, protein 1 g, fat 6 g, sodium 237 mg, sugar 4 g.

STUFFED MUSHROOMS

Makes 16

These are quite different from those bready baked stuffed mushrooms that were found on the banquet and party circuit for years. The mushrooms are cooked and then covered with a fresh tomato mix. You can prepare both the mushrooms and the tomatoes ahead of time and then fill whenever the snack-urge hits you.

16 large button mushrooms, cleaned with stems removed

4 tablespoons extra virgin olive oil

450 g (1 lb) tomatoes, peeled, seeded, and chopped, or well-drained canned chopped tomatoes

1 bunch spring onions, trimmed and chopped

1 clove garlic, peeled and chopped

1 tablespoon chopped basil

4 tablespoons chopped chives

1 teaspoon lemon juice

Salt and pepper

Parmesan for shaving, optional

Preheat the oven to 180ºC/350ºF/Gas Mark 4.

Line a small baking sheet with parchment paper. Lay the mushrooms on the paper, stem side up. Drizzle ½ teaspoon olive oil over each mushroom. Transfer to the preheated oven and roast for about 15 minutes or just until barely cooked through and coloring slightly. Remove from the oven and set aside to cool.

Combine the tomatoes with the spring onions, garlic, and basil in the bowl of a food processor fitted with a metal blade. Process, using quick on and off turns, for just a second or two. You want the mixture to blend, but not purée.

Scrape the mixture into a mixing bowl. Stir in the remaining olive oil along with the chives, lemon juice, salt, and pepper. Let marinate for about 15 minutes to allow the flavors to marry.

When ready to serve, drain the tomato mixture well in a fine mesh sieve. Mound an equal portion into each mushroom. If using, shave a piece of Parmesan over the top and serve.

Nutritional Analysis per Serving (1 mushroom): calories 39, carbohydrates 2 g, fiber 0 g, protein 1 g, fat 4 g, sodium 39 mg, sugar 1 g.

MARINATED ALMOND MUSHROOMS

Makes about 285 g (10 oz)

You will usually find marinated mushrooms flavored with Italian herbs and spices, while this version sings of the south of France, where blossoming almond trees herald the early spring. They are a light and appealing have-on-hand snack for any time of the year.

225 g (8 oz) button mushrooms, quartered

50 g (1¾ oz) toasted flaked almonds

125 ml (4 fl oz) almond oil

2 tablespoons sherry vinegar

1 tablespoon torn mint leaves

Salt and white pepper

Combine the mushrooms with the almonds in a mixing bowl. Add the oil, vinegar, and mint, stirring to blend. Season with salt and white pepper, cover, and let marinate for at least 1 hour before serving.

Store, covered and refrigerated, for up to 1 week. Serve at room temperature.

Nutritional Analysis per Serving (2 tablespoons): calories 41, carbohydrates 1 g, fiber 0 g, protein 1 g, fat 4 g, sodium 58 mg, sugar 0 g.

CAULIFLOWER "HUMMUS"

Makes about 1 liter (1¾ pints)

Here's our old friend cauliflower working its magic again. Its sweet, mellow flavor is just the right complement for the rich tahini. Raw or cooked vegetables cut into dipping-size sticks or rounds are great for dipping. This "hummus" can also be thinned down with a bit of Chicken Stock (see page 33) to make a sauce for grilled vegetables or even a chicken breast or fish fillet.

1 head cauliflower, trimmed and broken into small florets

2 tablespoons extra virgin olive oil

3 cloves garlic

Juice of 1 lemon

Freshly grated zest of 1 orange

125 ml (4 fl oz) tahini

1 teaspoon ground cumin

Tabasco sauce or to taste

½ teaspoon salt

Preheat the oven to 230ºC/450ºF/Gas Mark 8.

Line a roasting tray with parchment paper. Set aside.

Place the cauliflower in a medium mixing bowl and add the olive oil, tossing to coat well. Transfer the oiled cauliflower to the prepared roasting tray and place in the preheated oven. Roast, turning occasionally, for about 20 minutes or until lightly colored and tender.

Remove from the oven and place in the bowl of a food processor fitted with a metal blade. Add the garlic, lemon juice, orange zest, tahini, cumin, and Tabasco and process to a smooth, thick purée. Season with salt to taste and process to incorporate.

Serve immediately or scrape into a nonreactive container, cover, and refrigerate for up to 1 week. Serve at room temperature.

Nutritional Analysis per Serving (2 tablespoons): calories 37, carbohydrates 2 g, fiber 1 g, protein 1 g, fat 3 g, sodium 82 mg, sugar 0 g.

AUBERGINE-WALNUT DIP

Makes about 500 ml (17 fl oz)

This interesting mix works well with both raw and cooked vegetables, both as a dip and as a sauce. It keeps very well for a couple of weeks (covered and refrigerated) so it's an excellent make-ahead snack source.

450 g (1 lb) aubergines, trimmed and cut, lengthwise, into 5-mm
(¼-inch) thick slices

3 tablespoons walnut oil plus more if necessary

4 tablespoons extra virgin olive oil

450 g (1 lb) onion, peeled and chopped

1 tablespoon chopped garlic

140 g (5 oz) pecorino romano cheese, cut into small pieces

150 g (5¼ oz) toasted walnuts

85 g (3 oz) basil leaves

1 tablespoon balsamic vinegar

Salt and pepper

Preheat the grill and oil the grill pan.

Generously brush both sides of the aubergine slices with walnut oil. Place in a single layer under the grill about 7.5 cm (3 inches) from the heat. Grill for 4 minutes or until golden brown. Turn and grill the remaining side for another 4 minutes or until golden. If the aubergine seems to be dry, brush with additional walnut oil as it cooks. Remove from the grill and allow to cool. This may have to be done in batches, depending upon the size of your grill.

Heat the olive oil in a large frying pan over medium heat. Add the onion and garlic and cook, stirring frequently, for about 12 minutes or until golden brown.

Scrape the onion mixture into the bowl of a food processor fitted with a metal blade. Add the cooled aubergine along with the cheese, walnuts, basil, and vinegar. Season with salt and pepper to taste and process until almost smooth. Do not purée.

Scrape the mixture into a serving bowl and serve with vegetables for dipping.

Nutritional Analysis per Serving (2 tablespoons): calories 176, carbohydrates 6 g, fiber 2 g, protein 7 g, fat 15 g, sodium 180 mg, sugar 2 g.

DESSERTS

Enjoying a little sweetness after a hearty meal is very much a part of our culture. Just because you're significantly reducing your sugar intake doesn't mean you can't find a satisfying dessert using ingredients like dark chocolate, coconut, and nut butters. Here are just a few ideas to satisfy that sweet tooth. Of course, the simplest thing to do is to break off a piece of rich dark (over 70% cacao) chocolate and nibble away, but once in a while you might want a bit more to chew on in this department. I think you will find that all of these desserts are up to the challenge. Just remember indulgence is just that – it is not something that should be in your daily routine.

Coconut Bursts
Chocolate-Dipped Almonds
Coconut-Cashew Bars
Chocolate-Hazelnut Truffles
Chocolate Almond Cake
Chocolate Avocado Pudding
Lemon Soufflé Pudding
Baked Custard
Floating Island
Raw Chia Seed Pudding
Almond Meal Crêpes with Roasted Squash
Coconut-Lime Granita

COCONUT BURSTS

Makes about 36

This recipe couldn't be easier or a more perfect *Grain Brain* dessert. It also works as a super late-afternoon pick-me-up. You can use any toasted nut in place of the coconut or combine nuts with the coconut if you like.

225 g (8 oz) plain (at least 70% cacao) chocolate, chopped
55 g (2 oz) toasted coconut flakes

Line a baking sheet with greaseproof paper. Set aside.

Place the chocolate in the top half of a double boiler set over boiling water. Heat, stirring frequently, for about 5 minutes or until the chocolate is almost melted. Remove from the heat and beat until completely melted.

Add the coconut and stir to combine.

Drop the mixture by the spoonful onto the greaseproof paper on the prepared baking sheet. Set aside to cool and firm up.

When firm, serve or store, airtight, in layers separated by grease-proof paper, for up to 2 weeks.

Nutritional Analysis per Serving (1 piece): calories 50, carbohydrates 4 g, fiber 1 g, protein 1 g, fat 4 g, sodium 1 mg, sugar 2 g.

CHOCOLATE-DIPPED ALMONDS

Makes 450 g (1 lb)

Here is another simple to make, delightful treat. Just remember to buy really excellent chocolate – it will take these nuts from ordinary to extraordinary. If you think you are going to make these often it helps to have an inexpensive chocolate dipping fork on hand. They are available at many confectionery supply stores or online.

450 g (1 lb) unblanched almonds

225 g (8 oz) plain (at least 70% cacao) chocolate, chopped

Preheat the oven to 150ºC/300ºF/Gas Mark 2.

Line a baking sheet with greaseproof paper. Set aside.

Line a baking tray with parchment paper. Spread the almonds out in a single layer on the baking tray. Transfer to the preheated oven and toast for about 15 minutes or until golden brown and aromatic.

Remove from the oven and allow to cool.

Place the chocolate in the top half of a double boiler set over boiling water. Heat, stirring frequently, for about 5 minutes or until the chocolate is almost melted. Remove from the heat and beat until completely melted.

Working with one almond at a time, dip either one end or the whole almond into the chocolate, allowing excess to drop off. If dipping one end, you'll have to hold the nut in your fingertips; if the whole nut, lay it on a kitchen fork and dip it into the chocolate.

Place the chocolate-coated nut on the greaseproof-paper-lined sheet and set aside to harden.

When hardened, serve or store, airtight, in layers separated by greaseproof paper, for up to 2 weeks.

Nutritional Analysis per Serving (3 pieces): calories 28, carbohydrates 2 g, fiber 1 g, protein 1 g, fat 2 g, sodium 0 mg, sugar 1 g.

COCONUT-CASHEW BARS

Makes about 16

A bit between a chocolate and a cookie, these rich bars are an unexpected and satisfying treat. You can change the flavor by changing the nut butter and the nut garnish.

75 g (2³/₄ oz) shredded unsweetened coconut

115 g (4 oz) cashew butter

2 tablespoons almond meal

2 tablespoons coconut oil, melted

1 tablespoon stevia

1 teaspoon pure vanilla extract

115 g (4 oz) plain (at least 70% cacao) chocolate, chopped

75 g (2³/₄ oz) toasted cashew pieces

Preheat the oven to 160ºC/325ºF/Gas Mark 3.

Line the bottom of a 20-cm (8-inch) square baking tin with parchment paper. Set aside.

Combine the coconut with the cashew butter, almond meal, coconut oil, stevia, and vanilla in the bowl of a standing electric mixer fitted with a paddle. Beat on low for about 4 minutes or until the mixture has blended completely.

Using a rubber spatula, spread the coconut mixture out in the prepared baking tin, smoothing the top out evenly. Transfer to the preheated oven and bake for about 12 minutes or just until the edges begin to pull away from the tin and color slightly.

Remove from the oven and place on a wire rack to cool.

Place the chocolate in the top half of a double boiler set over boiling water. Heat, stirring frequently, for about 5 minutes or until the chocolate is almost melted. Remove from the heat and beat until completely melted.

Pour the melted chocolate over the cooled coconut mixture, smoothing the top with a rubber spatula. Sprinkle the cashew pieces evenly over the top and set aside to harden.

When firm, using a serrated knife, cut into bars. When hardened, serve or store, airtight, in layers separated by greaseproof paper, for up to 1 week.

Nutritional Analysis per Serving (1 bar): calories 169, carbohydrates 9 g, fiber 2 g, protein 3 g, fat 14 g, sodium 3 mg, sugar 3 g.

CHOCOLATE-HAZELNUT TRUFFLES

Makes about 50 pieces

These truffles are beautiful to look at and a very special treat. Although we use hazelnuts here, don't hesitate to use other nuts or even a variety of nuts with one batch of the chocolate ganache. Macadamia nuts would make an interesting choice. If you do use other nuts, replace the hazelnut extract with pure vanilla extract.

225 g (8 oz) plain (at least 70% cacao) chocolate, finely chopped

125 ml (4 fl oz) double cream

1 teaspoon hazelnut extract

Approximately 50 toasted hazelnuts

55 g (2 oz) sifted dark cocoa powder

Place the chocolate in a heatproof bowl set over very hot water.

Place the cream in a small saucepan over low heat and cook just until bubbles appear around the edge of the pan. Remove from the heat and pour the hot cream over the melting chocolate. Let sit for about 30 seconds. Add the extract and, using a wooden spoon, begin beating the cream into the chocolate. When completely blended, set aside to cool.

When cool, cover and refrigerate for 2 hours or until well chilled.

Line a baking tray with greaseproof paper. Set aside.

Place the cocoa powder (or finely chopped nuts) in a large shallow bowl or a plate. Set aside.

Using a small melon-baller or your hands, scoop up a small amount (no more than about 1 teaspoon) of the chocolate. Push a toasted hazelnut into the chocolate ganache and then reform the chocolate into a small, evenly shaped ball surrounding the nut.

Drop the ball into the cocoa powder (or nuts) and lightly toss to coat. Transfer to the greaseproof-paper-lined baking tray and continue making truffles.

When all of the truffles have been made, store, refrigerated, tightly covered in layers separated by greaseproof paper, for up to 1 week.

NOTE You can roll the truffles in about 150 g (5 oz) very finely chopped hazelnuts, but this will change the nutritional analysis substantially.

Nutritional Analysis per Serving (1 piece): calories 44, carbohydrates 3 g, fiber 1 g, protein 1 g, fat 4 g, sodium 1 mg, sugar 2 g.

CHOCOLATE ALMOND CAKE

Makes a 23-cm (9-inch) cake (about 12 servings)

This is far from an everyday treat, but it is an excellent cake to make when entertaining and you wish to offer your guests a scrumptious *Grain Brain* delicacy. A small scoop of mascarpone cheese on each wedge is the icing on the cake.

115 g (4 oz) butter, at room temperature, plus more for buttering
   the pan

175 g (6 oz) plain (at least 70% cacao) chocolate, chopped

175 g (6 oz) blanched raw almonds

100 g (3½ oz) stevia

3 tablespoons almond meal

2 teaspoons pure vanilla extract

6 large eggs, at room temperature

75 g (2¾ oz) chopped almonds

Preheat the oven to 180ºC/350ºF/Gas Mark 4.

Lightly coat the bottom and sides of a 23-cm (9-inch) springform pan with butter and then line it with parchment paper. Set aside.

Combine the chocolate and butter in the top half of a double boiler set over boiling water. Heat, stirring frequently, for about 5 minutes or until melted and completely blended. Remove from the heat and set aside.

Place the almonds and 2 tablespoons of the stevia in the bowl of a food processor fitted with a metal blade and process until it resembles coarse sand. Do not overprocess or the nuts will turn to butter. Scrape the almond mixture into the chocolate along with the almond meal, stirring to blend well.

Place the eggs in the bowl of a standing electric mixer fitted with the balloon whip. Add the remaining stevia and beat for about 7 minutes or until light yellow and tripled in volume.

Remove the bowl from the mixer and carefully fold the chocolate mixture into the eggs until there is no evidence of egg.

Pour the batter into the prepared pan and place in the preheated oven. Bake for 15 minutes; then sprinkle the chopped almonds over the top. Continue to bake for another 15 minutes or until the cake is set in the center.

Remove from the oven and place on a wire rack to cool for 45 minutes. Then, run a knife around the edge to ensure that the cake will easily come away from the sides. Remove the outside ring.

Transfer the cake to a cake plate and set aside to cool completely before cutting into small wedges and serving.

Nutritional Analysis per Serving (1 slice): calories 310, carbohydrates 13 g, fiber 4 g, protein 9 g, fat 27 g, sodium 36 mg, sugar 6 g.

CHOCOLATE AVOCADO PUDDING

Serves 4

Don't be shy . . . this really does make a tasty pudding. You need soft ripe avocados with no brown spots and excellent dark (more than 70% cacao) cocoa powder to achieve phenomenal texture and flavor.

2 avocados, peeled, pitted, and cut into pieces

125 ml (4 fl oz) unsweetened almond milk

40 g (1½ oz) dark cocoa powder

3 tablespoons liquid stevia

25 g (1 oz) almond butter

1 teaspoon pure vanilla extract

16 raspberries, optional

Combine the avocados with the almond milk, cocoa powder, stevia, almond butter, and vanilla in the bowl of a food processor fitted with a metal blade. Process until smooth.

Spoon the "pudding" into small serving bowls and serve garnished with a few raspberries, if desired.

Nutritional Analysis per Serving: calories 245, carbohydrates 14 g, fiber 9 g, protein 5 g, fat 21 g, sodium 48 mg, sugar 2 g.

LEMON SOUFFLÉ PUDDING

Serves 6

This is a very light dessert that looks spectacular. It can be served warm or covered and refrigerated for up to 8 hours for a chilled dish. Rather than used simply as topping, the berries can also be folded into the pudding.

3 large eggs, separated

75 g (2³/₄ oz) stevia

3 tablespoons tapioca starch

Pinch salt

Juice of 2 lemons

Freshly grated zest of 1 lemon

55 g (2 oz) butter, cut into small pieces

1 teaspoon vanilla extract

150 g (5 oz) berries, optional

Place the egg yolks in a small mixing bowl and beat to loosen. Set aside.

Place the egg whites in a large mixing bowl and using a hand-held electric mixer beat until stiff peaks form. Set aside.

Combine the stevia, tapioca starch, and salt in a saucepan. Add 450 ml (³/₄ pint) cold water, whisking to blend completely. Place over medium heat and cook, stirring constantly, until thickened. Stir in the lemon juice and zest.

Stir about 4 tablespoons of the lemon mixture into the egg yolks to temper. Then, stir the warm egg yolk mixture into the lemon mixture. Add the butter and vanilla and continue to cook, stirring constantly, until blended and thick.

Remove from the heat and fold the hot lemon pudding into the egg whites. Continue to fold until the egg whites are completely blended and the pudding is light and fluffy.

Spoon into individual serving dishes, top with a few berries, if desired, and serve.

Nutritional Analysis per Serving: calories 133, carbohydrates 9 g, fiber 1 g, protein 3 g, fat 10 g, sodium 33 mg, sugar 4 g.

BAKED CUSTARD

Serves 6

This is about as close to an old-fashioned custard as you can get without using lots of cream and sugar. Although it can be served warm, the flavors will be more pronounced if allowed to cool or, even better, refrigerated until chilled. The vanilla seeds add a depth of sweetness that vanilla extract alone will not give to the finished dish.

About 15 g (½ oz) unsalted butter, at room temperature for
    buttering dish(es)
600 ml (1 pint) unsweetened almond milk
125 ml (4 fl oz) double cream
4 large eggs

2 large egg yolks

Seeds from $1/2$ vanilla bean

75 g ($2^3/_4$ oz) stevia

2 teaspoons pure vanilla extract

Pinch salt

Preheat the oven to 180ºC/350ºF/Gas Mark 4.

Generously butter 6 x 125-ml (4 fl oz) custard dishes or a 1.5-liter ($2^1/_2$-pint) baking dish. Set aside.

Combine the almond milk and double cream in a small saucepan over medium-low heat and cook for about 4 minutes or until very hot but not yet simmering. Remove from the heat.

Combine the whole eggs and egg yolks with the vanilla seeds, stevia, vanilla extract, and salt, stirring to blend. Don't whip or the eggs will get foamy and the bubbles will remain on the top of the baked custard. Strain the eggs through a medium-fine mesh sieve into a clean container. (This is not essential, but it does strain out the bits of egg white that coagulate.)

Stirring constantly, add about 4 tablespoons of the hot milk to the eggs to temper. Then, slowly stir in the remaining milk.

Place the buttered dishes (or dish) in a pan large enough to hold them. Add cold water to come about halfway up the sides of the dishes. (The water bath is extremely important as it keeps the outside of the custard from cooking too fast, leaving the center undone.) Transfer to the preheated oven and bake for about 25 minutes (35 for the larger dish) or until almost set in the center. It should still sway when the dishes are moved. To test, poke a small clean knife into the center; if it comes out clean the custard is ready to be removed from the oven.

Remove from the oven and carefully transfer the dishes to a wire rack to finish cooking and cool slightly before serving.

Nutritional Analysis per Serving: calories 155, carbohydrates 4 g, fiber 1 g, protein 6 g, fat 13 g, sodium 225 mg, sugar 1 g.

FLOATING ISLAND

Serves 4

Floating Island is a classic French dessert (known as oeufs à la neige) that is rarely made anymore. It is quite uncomplicated to make and yet looks difficult when it all comes together. This version is not as sweet as the classic and is fragrant with almond rather than the usual vanilla.

3 extra large eggs, at room temperature

50 g (1³/₄ oz) stevia

500 ml (17 fl oz) unsweetened almond milk

1 teaspoon almond extract

75 g (2³/₄ oz) assorted berries, optional

2 tablespoons toasted flaked almonds, optional

Separate 2 of the eggs.

Place the 2 egg whites in the bowl of a standing electric mixer fitted with a balloon whisk and beat on medium for about 3 minutes or until soft peaks form. Slowly add 2 tablespoons of the stevia and continue to beat until the whites are stiff, but not dry.

Heat the almond milk in a large frying pan over medium heat. Cook for about 4 minutes or until bubbles form around the edge of the pan. Using a large spoon, scoop up a large, rounded mound of egg white and drop it into the hot milk. Continue until you have used up all of the egg whites; you should have enough to make 4 or, at the most, 5 floating meringues.

Bring the milk to a very gentle simmer and cook the meringues for about 5 minutes or just until cooked through and a bit firm. Do not discard the milk.

Using a slotted spoon, transfer the meringues from the milk to a plate, allowing excess liquid to drop off. If still wet, pat the bottom of the meringue with kitchen paper. When well drained, transfer the meringues to a dry plate and refrigerate while you make the sauce.

Pour the hot poaching milk into a medium saucepan over medium-low heat.

Combine the egg yolks with the remaining egg and stevia, whisking to blend thoroughly. Add a bit of the hot milk to the egg mixture and when blended, whisk it into the hot milk in the saucepan. Cook, stirring constantly, for about 10 minutes or until the custard coats the back of a spoon. Stir in the almond extract and remove from the heat.

Place the saucepan in a bowl of iced water and stir frequently to chill. Pour into a shallow serving bowl, cover the top with greaseproof paper (to keep a film from forming), and refrigerate for at least 30 minutes or until cold.

When ready to serve, remove the greaseproof paper and float the chilled meringues in the custard. Sprinkle a few berries and almonds over the custard, if desired, and serve.

Nutritional Analysis per Serving: calories 105, carbohydrates 6 g, fiber 1 g, protein 6 g, fat 7 g, sodium 139 mg, sugar 3 g.

RAW CHIA SEED PUDDING

Serves 4

This easy-to-make pudding can also be made with coconut milk, which is a bit richer in flavor than almond milk. You can also add 2 tablespoons dark cocoa powder and a pinch of cinnamon for chocolate pudding. Chia seed pudding does, however, need to rest for a number of hours; if the chia seeds have not soaked long enough, they will cause a bit of stomach upset.

500 ml (17 fl oz) unsweetened almond milk

15 g (½ oz) almond butter

1 tablespoon stevia

1 teaspoon almond or pure vanilla extract

75 g (2³/₄ oz) chia seeds

55 g (2 oz) blueberries, optional

Combine the almond milk, almond butter, stevia, and almond extract in a blender jar and process until smooth. Add the chia seeds and process to just blend. The whirl in the blender helps keep the seeds from clumping together.

Pour into 1 large or 4 small serving bowls. Cover and refrigerate for 30 minutes; then, stir to make sure the seeds are evenly distributed. Again, cover and refrigerate for 8 hours or overnight.

Serve chilled, with a few berries on top, if desired.

Nutritional Analysis per Serving: calories 160, carbohydrates 14 g, fiber 9 g, protein 5 g, fat 10 g, sodium 103 mg, sugar 2 g.

ALMOND MEAL CRÊPES WITH ROASTED SQUASH

Makes about 8

This dessert has its origins in the classic French Crêpes Suzette, but here the crêpes reflect the *Grain Brain* diet. Roasted squash may seem like an odd dessert choice, but most squash are inherently sweet and, when roasted, the caramelization makes them even more so.

The crêpes are quite fragile so you should transfer them from the pan straight to the serving dish or plate. For an elegant end-of-the-meal treat they can be topped with a dollop of mascarpone and a few berries and/or a drizzle of melted dark chocolate. However they are also quite tasty plain.

340 g (12 oz), such as butternut, peeled and cut into 1-cm (¹/₂-inch) cubes

2 teaspoons coconut oil plus more for cooking

100 g (3¹/₂ oz) almond meal

2 large eggs

4 tablespoons unsweetened almond milk

25 g (1 oz) butter, melted

1 teaspoon stevia

1 teaspoon pure vanilla extract

4 tablespoons soda water

¼ cup chopped toasted almonds, optional

Preheat the oven to 190ºC/375ºF/Gas Mark 5.

Toss the squash with the coconut oil and place on a small roasting tray. Transfer to the preheated oven and roast, tossing occasionally, for about 15 minutes or until golden brown and cooked through. Remove from the oven and keep warm while you make the crêpes. (You can also roast the squash ahead of time and reheat when ready to serve.)

Place the almond meal in a medium mixing bowl.

In a separate bowl, whisk the eggs, almond milk, butter, stevia, and vanilla together. Add the almond milk mixture to the almond meal, beating to combine. When blended, stir in the soda water.

Lightly coat a nonstick crêpe pan with coconut oil and place over medium-low heat.

Using a ladle, transfer about 4 tablespoons of the batter to the hot pan, carefully spreading it out to form a thin pancake. Cook for about 90 seconds or until firm and golden brown on the bottom. Carefully flip the crêpe and cook for another minute or until set and golden brown. If desired, as finished you can stack the crêpes on a warm plate, separating each one by a piece of greaseproof paper to keep them from sticking together.

Continue making crêpes until all of the batter has been used.

Serve with a spoonful of roasted squash in the center of each crêpe and, if desired, a sprinkle of toasted almonds.

Nutritional Analysis per Serving (1 crêpe): calories 113, carbohydrates 5 g, fiber 2 g, protein 3 g, fat 10 g, sodium 23 mg, sugar 1 g.

COCONUT-LIME GRANITA

Makes about 6 x 50-ml (2 fl oz) servings

Granita is certainly not ice cream, but it is a refreshing treat none-theless. It is nice to have on hand for a last-minute dessert.

375 ml (13 fl oz) coconut milk

2 tablespoons lime juice

2 tablespoons liquid stevia

Combine the coconut milk, lime juice, and stevia in a medium bowl. When blended, stir in 250 ml (8 fl oz) cold water. Pour into a shallow container and place in the freezer.

Freeze for at least 3 hours or until completely frozen.

Using a kitchen fork, scrape back and forth over the top to shave the granite into flakes. Serve immediately. Any remaining granita will keep, frozen, for up to 2 weeks.

Nutritional Analysis per Serving: calories 53, carbohydrates 2 g, fiber 0 g, protein 0 g, fat 5 g, sodium 7 mg, sugar 0 g.

Acknowledgments

Just as I was beginning to celebrate the success of *Grain Brain*, the demand for a cookbook plunged me quickly back into writing mode with another cadre of creative, indefatigable individuals who helped me put this together. And once again I found myself at the mercy of experts in the publishing sphere (especially those with more experience than I in the kitchen to craft recipes worthy of publication) who made it all happen seamlessly – and deliciously.

First, I must collectively thank all the scientists and fellow colleagues who've gone before me in exploring the health and functionality of the human brain and whose research has informed the lessons and dietary recommendations I write about today. Thanks also to my patients who are often my greatest sources of new knowledge.

Thank you to Bonnie Solow, my friend and literary agent who has been with me since day one in helping me promulgate my message about the true path to optimal brain health. You've been a steadfast champion in my mission to end brain disease and I am forever grateful for the opportunities you've provided. If it weren't for your insights, patience, gracious leadership, and attention to details, we might never have gotten the chance to pen this important culinary guide.

To Judie Choate, my kitchen comrade in creating an exquisite menu of options. Indeed, as a notable chef, writer, and "pioneer in the promotion of American food," you were essential in the process of meeting my guidelines while never losing an ounce of flavor. And to your husband, Steve Pool, who brought these meals to life with his beautiful photography.

To Kristin Loberg, my *Grain Brain* collaborator, who helped to ensure the continuity of my writing as we shifted to this cookbook. As before, while the content of my information represents my research and professional experience, it is wholly through your wordsmithing that I can convey my message to a broad readership.

To the tireless team at Little, Brown that has been a partner with me in so many ways. I bow down to Michael Pietsch, Reagan Arthur, Heather Fain, Miriam Parker, Nicole Dewey, Cathy Gruhn, Tracy Williams, Andy LeCount, Jean Garnett, and especially my editor, Tracy Behar, who combed through every sentence with her knack for keeping everything succinct and clear. It has been and remains a pleasure to work with such a dedicated, professional group. To James Murphy, Andrew Luer, and John D'Orazio of Proton Enterprises for your incredible skill in seeing the big picture from a management perspective.

To Digital Natives, my savvy tech team responsible for making my website come alive as a companion to my books.

To my wife, Leize. Thank you for all the time and commitment in lovingly preparing the recipes. I am grateful beyond measure to have you in my life.

Index

oils 11, 25
olives: braised lamb shanks with green
   olives 159–60
   caponata 105–6
   chicken with lemon and olives
      185–6
   Greek salad 78
   marinated 230–1
   tapenade 42–3
omega-3 fats 12
omega-6 fats 12
omelette, roasted onion 55–7
onions: cabbage and onion braise
   116–17
   calves liver and onions 152–3
   roasted onion omelette 55–7
   sun-dried tomato and onion chutney
      55–8
   sweet spice onion jam 163–4
   tomato-onion salsa 148–50
orange juice 8

pancakes: almond meal crepes with
   roasted squash 254–5
   courgette pancakes 54–5
pancetta: Brussels sprouts with
   pancetta and sage 112
   warm Swiss chard, pancetta and
      almond salad 83–4
parsley: lemon-parsley butter 132
pâté, chicken liver 232–3
peppers: turkey steaks with roasted
   peppers and cheese 188
pesto-roasted chicken 173–5
pistachios, butternut squash with
   spinach and 126–7
plantains: fried green plantains
   (tostones) 125–6
pork 28
   adobo pork 167–8
   curried pork stew 72–3

grilled pork chops with salsa verde
   165
Gruyère-glazed pork chops 166–7
meatloaf stuffed with hard-boiled
   eggs 145–6
pork fillet with sweet spice onion
   jam 163–4
slow-roasted spareribs 169–70
stir-fried pork with watercress 168–9
stuffed pork loin 162–3
Tex-Mex cowboy beef burgers
   148–9
Thai pork lettuce cups 82–3
Portuguese-style sardines 204–5
poultry 28, 171–90
prawns: garlic prawns 206
   prawn and celery salad 85–6
   prawn creole 207
   tomatoes stuffed with prawn salad
      84–5
prosciutto: courgette casserole with
   prosciutto and cheese 128
proteins 28
pumpkin seeds 26
   crunchy pumpkin seed toss 222–3
   roast pumpkin seeds 221
   spinach with spring onions and
      pumpkin seeds 115

radicchio, grilled 115–16
radishes braised in butter 121–2
relish, jicama-cucumber 175–7
ricotta cheese: pesto-roasted chicken
   173–5
   quick 'moussaka' 160–1
   torta rustica 60–1
rise and shine shake 47–8
rocket: green mango, watercress and
   rocket salad 73–4
   grilled veal chops with rocket
      150–1

Author Biography

David Perlmutter, MD, is a Board-Certified Neurologist and Fellow of the American College of Nutrition who received his M.D. degree from the University of Miami School of Medicine, where he was awarded the Leonard G. Rowntree Research Award. He is president of the Perlmutter Health Center in Naples, Florida, and the co-founder and president of The Perlmutter BrainFoundation. Dr. Perlmutter serves as a Volunteer Associate Professor at the University of Miami School of Medicine. He is a frequent lecturer at symposia sponsored by such medical institutions as Columbia University, the University of Arizona, Scripps Institute, New York University, and Harvard University. Dr. Perlmutter has been interviewed on many nationally syndicated radio and television programs, including 20/20, Larry King Live, CNN, Fox News, Fox & Friends, The Today Show, Oprah, The CBS Early Show, and The Dr. Oz Show, where he serves as Medical Advisor. In 2002 Dr. Perlmutter was the recipient of the Linus Pauling Award for his innovative approaches to neurological disorders and in addition was awarded the Denham Harmon Award for his pioneering work in the application of free radical science to clinical medicine. He is the recipient of the 2006 National Nutritional Foods Association Clinician of the Year Award as well as the 2010 Humanitarian of the Year Award from the American College of Nutrition. He has contributed extensively to the world medical literature, with publications appearing in *The Journal of Neurosurgery*, *The Southern Medical*

Journal, *Journal of Applied Nutrition*, and *Archives of Neurology*. He is the author of seven books, including the #1 *New York Times* bestseller *Grain Brain*. Dr. Perlmutter serves as Editor-in-Chief of the peer-reviewed scientific journal, *Brain and Gut*.

books to help you live a good life

Join the conversation and tell
us how you live a #goodlife

🐦 @yellowkitebooks
📘 YellowKiteBooks
📌 Yellow Kite Books
📷 YellowKiteBooks